IT'S OK

to

FAIL THE

TEST

IT'S OK

to

FAIL THE

TEST

As Long as You Learn the Lesson!

Name David Craig

Pleasant Word
A Division of WinePress Group

Pleasant Word (a division of WinePress Publishing, PO Box 428, Enumclaw, WA 98022) functions only as book publisher. As such, the ultimate design, content, editorial accuracy, and views expressed or implied in this work are those of the author.

ISBN 13: 978-1-4141-1441-5
ISBN 10: 1-4141-1441-9
Library of Congress Catalog Card Number: 2009903412

For anyone who has faced tragedy in life
– or anyone who might.

CONTENTS

BEFORE WORDS

"… those who become Christians become new persons. They
are not the same anymore, for the old life is gone.
A new life has begun!"
—2 Corinthians 5:17 NLT

IT HAS BEEN said, "The greatest teacher is a good student." I know this to be true because I teach—I am a surgeon who trains surgeons. Where medicine is concerned, however, the greatest healer is Jesus Christ—the Great Physician. I believe that being an instrument of God's healing power holds the greatest value and purpose for any faithful physician. The book you are about to read validates that belief. It was written by one of my patients. As you will see in the chapters that follow, his faith has served to remind me how big God really is, how much He loves us, and how many different ways He will use to call us to Himself.

Physicians have a lot of reasons to believe they are the source of healing. But show me one doctor who gave himself even the least of his skills: dexterity, insight, or the capacity to anticipate unusual disease. These are all gifts from God. A patient who comes into a physician's life and brings this reality into focus is likewise a gift from God. David Craig is such a patient.

When I first met David, I was amazed by two things. First, he had survived a disease called cancer for years longer than expected; second, he had deftly orchestrated his own care far outside the mainstream of typical medical management. I've always seen myself as someone ready, willing, and able to push the envelope. However, the chronic nature of David's disease and the treatment he applied to it wasn't simply pushing the envelope. It was in another realm completely!

Creation is intrinsically miraculous. But there are other types of events that strain the bounds of medical/physical credulity. David's medical condition, recovery, and response to an array of treatments are evidence of such events. Understand, dear reader, the biology of David's disease and the results he experienced are *not* medically typical. His experience is, to say the least, a medical anomaly—in a word, miraculous.

I am blessed to have been a part of David's story. But one particular challenge it presents is explaining to my colleagues why I would be willing to participate in the care of someone whose desire is *quality* of life and not maximum *quantity*. Actually, answering that question isn't the hard part. Rather, it's the response to my explanation that, "This man has no doubts about where he is going when he dies." Generally, I get a blank expression that asks, "What did you just say?"

David lacks the fear of death that leaves many—if not most—people with similar diagnoses grasping for extreme measures of care regardless of the potentially incapacitating side effects. The prognosis is generally something like this: "We might be able to cure your disease, Mr. Smith, giving you a one to two out of ten chance of survival for five years. The problem is you will need a hole in your neck to breathe through, you likely will not be able to speak again, and you will have to take all of your nutrition through a feeding tube directly connected to your stomach."

Not all scenarios are this bad. But for an unfortunate number, these side effects are permanent. David did his homework and his bookwork. As a result, he knew the limits of medical and surgical care for a Stage Four disease (the most advanced and deadly category). He knew the odds were low that conventional medicine could give him anything (chemotherapy, radiation, and/or surgery) that would actually cure him of cancer. He also knew that God would be with him no matter what care alternative he chose.

His refusal to accept conventionally applied treatments might make one think David was simply being indifferent to the seriousness of his disease. Such was not the case. Perhaps he thought fate had dealt him a bad hand and he would just have to play it out. His perspective was nothing of the kind. He knew that the same sovereign God who made the heavens also made the earth and David Craig with it. That same good and just God allowed him the experience of a disease called cancer not only to provide lessons about a relationship with him, but also with the assurance that he could leave this life without any doubts about where his final destination would be—with God for all eternity, whole and healed, missing no parts and never to suffer again.

That man came to see me in search of treatment alternatives, prayerful and full of grace; a real man, not a perfect one, but one after God's own heart. His case led me to attempt treatment options and approaches I never would have attempted otherwise, let alone try to defend.

David's story is only an excerpt of his life to this point in time. Apart from an omniscient God, no one knows what the future holds. Nevertheless, I believe any outcome will honor God and spread the message of his grace to those involved in this man's care. As a result, my practice will never be the same. I will personally never be the same.

—Paul F. Castellanos, MD, FCCP
Laryngology Bronchoesophagology
Associate Professor of Surgery
Division of Otolaryngology Head and Neck Surgery
University of Alabama at Birmingham
Birmingham, Alabama

Chapter One

IF ONLY I KNEW
HOW TO PRAY

"In the beginning the Word already existed.
He was with God, and he was God"
—John 1:1 NLT

THE ROOM IS small, L-shaped, mildly drab. A bank of windows on one wall provides the only daylight. Seven recliner-style chairs line two of the six walls. Beside each chair is a portable IV pole, able to hold from one to four separate bags of pharmaceutical fluids.

It's Wednesday, May 16, 2007. I am sitting in the third chair from the end, with George on my left and Karen on my right. Linda is across from me.

"Good morning, George. You're looking well."

"Hello, Karen. Will your husband be bringing you lunch today?"

Just noise, really; not conversation. Polite words used to break the monotonous silence; vocal camouflage for emotional and mental anguish. None of us believed we were at risk for this disease. Certainly none of us fully understands it.

Mary, a nurse, arrives to insert a butterfly catheter into the top of my hand. She encourages deep breaths for tolerating the needle stick. A blood draw determines white and red cell counts, and then the oncologist stops by to discuss this week's chemotherapy infusion. He apprises me of the side effects I can expect and offers help to counteract them. Finally, he writes a prescription for the drugs I will receive this day.

A short time later, Mary attaches to the catheter a thin tube connected to the clear plastic bag she hangs on my IV pole. A drug called Erbitux begins dripping into my body. Once the bag has emptied, Mary will attach another containing Taxol, followed by carboplatin, followed by Leucovorin, followed by fluorouracil (5-FU). This weekly process takes from four to six hours and is standard procedure for head and neck cancer patients here at the Seattle Cancer Treatment and Wellness Center.

The team at SCTWC is one of the most compassionate, caring, and considerate toward its patients. Nevertheless, this is the last place on earth I want to be right now—sitting in the group room having some of the most toxic substances developed by conventional medicine infused into my bloodstream—poisons created to kill rapidly developing abnormal cells without destroying the body's internal organs first.

Linda looks at me and asks, "So what are you in for?"

I begin to explain that I am now in my second week of a prescribed twelve-week chemotherapy regimen. The process will deliver fractionated doses of chemo to the cancerous tumor growing under the right side base of my tongue, extending down and behind the hyoid bone. "I've researched and tried many different cancer treatment methods since 1997," I offer, "including chemotherapy. At best, I've achieved no more than a reasonable plan for managing the disease."

Linda's small-cell lung cancer developed only recently. "Ten years!" she exclaims. "You've been battling cancer for ten years? I guess my problem isn't that big by comparison."

George and Karen are interested too. At present, I explain, surgery is not an acceptable treatment option for me. The cancerous mass has entwined itself around very important cranial nerves that control swallowing, speaking, and breathing. Complete surgical excision of the tumor would mean removing those nerves, leaving me permanently incapacitated. Previously infused chemotherapy drugs have left me with some kidney damage, vein loss, tonal loss in my right ear, and *tinnitus*—constant ringing—in both ears. I swore I would never again voluntarily poison my body. So why have I broken that self-made promise?

My medical team agrees that the best course of action is an attempt to shrink the tumor away from the cranial nerves, which may allow removal of any residual tumor by surgical means. My first and only thought upon hearing this recommendation was *Oh, no ... not again ... not chemotherapy!* Yet despite my previous stand never again to subject myself to the poisonous process of chemo, here I am, one more time.

As I answer queries from Linda, George, and Karen, I think about the questions I've asked myself so many times in the past: What did I do to deserve this lot in life? Do I really have the physical, emotional, mental, and spiritual strength to continue fighting this battle? Will I ever be rid of this horrible disease? What does God have planned for me this time?

How, exactly, did I get to this place in my life?

On a typically dreary, blustery October morning in the Pacific Northwest, I awoke with a raging sore throat. I tried the usual home and over-the-counter remedies, but the medicated mouthwashes, herbal teas, and throat lozenges did nothing to alleviate the pain. By week's end the severity of the pain prompted me to visit an urgent-care clinic near my home in Bellevue, Washington.

The physician on duty examined my throat, took a culture, and wrote out a prescription for an antibiotic. A subsequent call from the clinic confirmed that the culture was negative for strep. Good news, I thought. However, while the pain and soreness subsided within a week or so, I continued to experience the feeling of something caught in my throat. Attempts to expectorate this foreign object proved unsuccessful.

A week or so later, I became determined to remove from my throat whatever it was that might be lodged there. Leaning over the bathroom sink one particular morning, I retched as hard as I could. Blood filled my mouth and spilled into the sink, and my wife, witnessing this scene, said, "You *will* go see a doctor!"

I never liked doctors, hospitals, clinics, or medical facilities of any kind. Worst of all I hate needles! Like most men, I never went to the doctor until and unless the malady really started to interfere with my daily activities. But I made an appointment to visit the Bellevue Ear, Nose, and Throat Clinic. Dr. Daniel Seely found a large mass growing in the right side of my throat, just below the base of the tongue and just above the voice box.

The doctor asked about my family's medical history. My paternal grandparents and their siblings had all died of cancer.

Strike one.

Dr. Seely continued to probe. It seemed curious that an otherwise healthy forty-nine-year-old male would be at risk for such a growth. "Are you a drinker?" he asked.

"No."

"Smoker?"

"No."

"Have you been ingesting any toxic waste?"

The doctor was now even more puzzled as to the possible origin and growth rate of the mass. Such a tumor was found primarily in individuals who had been smoking and drinking for more than fifty years. I did not fit the profile.

Strike two.

Dr. Seely ordered a battery of tests, including an upper body X-ray, blood work, and an MRI.

The X-ray was normal, as was the blood work. The MRI, however, displayed a large growth with the appearance of a leech and about the size of a man's thumb, clinging to the lining on the right side of my throat. While the doctor offered some hope that the mass might be benign, only a biopsy could confirm or deny malignancy.

On November 4, 1997, I was admitted to the Overlake Surgical Center for biopsy surgery. When I awoke from the anesthesia, my wife and daughters were sitting next to my bed. Watching the tears fill their eyes, I did not have to guess the outcome. The doctor came into the room and said, "Mr. Craig, you have cancer. It's described as poorly differentiated squamous cell carcinoma, in its second stage."

Strike three.

Cancer! Only individuals who have experienced cancer or who have loved ones who have dealt with the disease can truly understand the inexplicable effect of such a pronouncement. Priorities change. Attitudes change. Relationships change. Everything, in fact, changes. At least it did for me. Here began a roller-coaster ride of emotion: horror and hope, despair and expectation, anger and anticipation, frustration and fear. Close behind came bitterness, emptiness, helplessness, and worst of all, hopelessness.

THERE'S ALWAYS PRAYER

Spiraling into the next stage of our emotional ride, my wife and I visited Dr. Seely to discuss various treatment options. "The first option," he explained, "and generally the best, is surgery."

He described the procedure as an *open resection*. Beginning with an incision at the center of the lower lip, he would continue cutting down and below the chin, then along and under the right jawbone up to the right ear. The flesh and muscle would be pulled away, allowing the jawbone to be broken and swung out away from the throat.

With the tumor site exposed, a scalpel would be used to cut around the tumor mass with the goal of achieving "clear margins." A large portion of the tongue base, as well as part of the larynx and surrounding muscle, would probably be removed. Tissue would be taken from a pectoral muscle and used to reinforce the tongue base to aid in swallowing after surgical recovery. A specialist would be called to assist with reconstruction of the jaw and neck.

"Have you got anything else, doc?" I asked.

In response, he offered the traditional, standard chemotherapy and radiation for treating base-of-tongue squamous cell carcinoma. Pursuit of this option would mean a visit to an oncologist for details of the process, side effects, and potential results.

"What if I do nothing?"

"Doing nothing is an option," Dr. Seely replied. "The tumor will continue to grow. Given its apparent rate of growth, it will slowly close off your throat and your ability to swallow and breathe. Based upon what we currently know about the disease, it will spread into your lymph system, probably into your lungs, and finally, you will die." Getting no response from us and observing our emotional state, he added softly, "You know, there's always prayer."

What? We had not anticipated that suggestion from the doctor. We quickly assured him that we, in fact, did believe in prayer. Once the news of my condition had spread to our friends and relatives, many had called to say they would be praying for us. We had both grown up in church and had been taught that prayer was the first line of defense against the evils of this world, including diseases such as cancer. We knew God was able to heal people of their diseases.

For the next few moments, as the conversation continued, I was only present physically, as if I were an outside observer. I had the feeling of watching myself act, while having no control over my actions.

Ironically, I'd been asked many times over the years to pray for friends or relatives who had cancer. I'd seen many church congregations pray for people with this dreaded disease. Within my frame of reference, however, I'd never seen anyone completely healed of cancer, and in fact, most had died. Why then, would God choose to heal *me*?

My parents were evangelical pastors for more than fifty years. As a preacher's kid, I attended church twice on Sunday and at least once during the week. I was saved—that is, I had experienced salvation at an early age. Whenever a visiting evangelist, a summer church-camp speaker, or Billy Graham gave an altar call, I got "saved" again. After high school I attended a Bible-based college in the Puget Sound area, where five years later I received the highest theological degree conferred by the school at that time. I had an abundance of head knowledge about God and all of his attributes, including healing, and yet—I no longer knew how to pray.

No, I hadn't forgotten the protocol for prayer, nor had I forgotten the words. The truth was I no longer had a relationship with the Word.

In the first chapter of his book on Christian apologetics, *Christianity on the Offense*, author Dan Story describes the prevalence in the West of a resurrected worldview that he calls a form of neo-deism. "Its adherents," he writes, "are people who claim to be Christian, who still profess to believe in the God of Scripture, and who identify culturally with Christianity; but these people live their lives as if God does not exist." Story then quotes George Barna's survey of religious views in America: "Large majorities of people now claim that the Bible and religion are very important in their lives, but there is little evidence that this change in attitude has influenced the way they live." Neo-deists, Story concludes, "are individuals who do not want to reject the Christian idea of a personal God ... but they want to preserve their sovereignty and independence from God."[1]

Without wanting to admit it, I knew my life fit the definition of a neo-deist perfectly. Oh, I hadn't simply decided one day to adopt such a worldview. I hadn't reached my spiritual condition overnight. Just as it had taken many months for the cancerous tumor in my throat to grow to the size of a man's thumb, so it had taken many years for the cancer of self-sufficiency to grow to a size in my life where there was no longer any room for God.

It started innocently enough (as it always does). Gradually, a healthy aspiration to succeed became an insatiable hunger for material possessions; little half-truths became big black lies; the desire for short-term pleasure became long-term bad behavior; an ever-increasing appetite for recreation replaced a hunger for the nourishment of God's Word. My heart had become hardened and detached from anyone or anything that did not serve my self-absorbed agenda.

Over a period of twenty-five years, I began to crave and finally demand my independence from God. The faith I had been taught to value—forgotten. The love relationship God wanted with me—forsaken. A call to ministry—abandoned.

Church and church-related activities had become an act—just for show. After all, I knew when to stand up, when to sit down, when to bow my head, and when to say amen. I knew the words to all the songs. I knew how to play church. I haughtily wore the label "Christian."

Suddenly awakened by the thoughts flashing before me, I mentally returned to Dr. Seely's examination room. Yes, I told myself, prayer would be the best treatment option—if only I knew how to pray!

So Few Options, So Little Time

Well-meaning friends, neighbors, relatives, and business associates all offered advice about my best course of treatment. Often unsolicited, this deluge of information only served to confuse and worsen the situation. So-called friends and long-lost relatives involved in various multilevel marketing organizations came out of nowhere and insisted we purchase the latest in natural remedies through their pyramid group. "Our product is the best cancer-fighting agent your money can buy," they promised. Why is it that well-intentioned people so often promise to *pray for* and then deem it permissible to *prey upon* the tragedy of friends? Is that what real friends do?

It was at this juncture that I recognized the necessity to take an active, empowering role in deciding the proper treatment of the cancer plaguing my body. This proved to be one of the most important decisions I would make.

A week or so after talking with Dr. Seely, we visited an oncologist in the Overlake Medical Center physicians group. As we expected, he assured us that the regimen he would prescribe would be the right one, the proven one, the effective one. Treatment would include six courses of chemotherapy consisting of a drug called cisplatin (one of the most toxic in the chemo-drug spectrum at that time), followed by another called fluorouracil (5-FU). The process included an overnight stay in the hospital for infusion of the cisplatin. Then I would be discharged with a catheter in my arm attached to a bag of 5-FU that would slowly drip into my body over the next twenty-four hours. Three additional bags of 5-FU would be infused in succession.

"The purpose of this chemotherapy regimen," said the oncologist, "is not necessarily to eradicate the tumor. Rather, its purpose is to prepare the tumor to receive radiation." The wholesale destruction of white blood cells by the cisplatin would most likely require a subsequent stay in the hospital for the infusion of antibiotics to preclude infection.

So ... kidney failure, pancreatic failure, even heart failure were all possibilities, but the drugs *might* shrink the tumor?

We were referred to yet another oncologist to discuss the process for radiation treatment. He described it as the bombardment of the tumor site with gamma rays twice a day, five days a week, for eight weeks. During this time the lining of the throat would become extremely sore. "Imagine your throat lining covered with chancre sores," he said. "The pain will be so severe you won't want to eat and you won't be able to sleep. We'll most likely have to admit you to the hospital to receive nourishment intravenously."

Wow! More great news. These guys were just full of pleasant surprises.

In addition to the short-term side effects of radiation, the doctor promised a permanent loss of facial hair and salivary function. To the first I said, "No big deal"; to the second, "Are you kidding me?" Suddenly I was not interested in being poisoned *and* burned, almost simultaneously. There was no way I was going to subject myself to chemo and radiation.

MEET THE WORD

As part of my new take-charge attitude, I spent many hours over the next couple of weeks using the Internet to explore new treatments, new techniques, new drugs, and even alternative (holistic and naturopathic) methods for cancer treatment. In an age of stem-cell research, satellite links, and DNA alteration, there had to be a newer, lower-morbidity silver bullet available for targeting a disease like the one in my throat. There had to be a more promising, less painful, and more acceptable means of treating cancer.

I rarely slept, compiling mounds of literature and other data. Many nights the questions, Why me? How could something like this possibly happen to me? interrupted my research. Yet deep inside my heart, when I was alone in the dark with my thoughts, I believed I knew at least one of the reasons why the cancer was there. On many of those same nights, I tried to pray, but my prayers seemed only to reach the ceiling and bounce back. What was the use?

During one seemingly endless night, dazed and blurry-eyed, my gaze fell upon a small cabinet in our family room. For no particular reason I opened it and looked inside. After pawing through a stack of books and magazines, I found a Bible given to me upon high school graduation some thirty years earlier. I picked it up and blew off the dust.

I opened the Bible. Where to start? I thumbed through the yellowed pages and stumbled upon passages I had underlined many years before:

> There is a way that seems right to a man, but in the end it leads to death.
>
> —Prov. 14:12

> Come now, let us reason together, says the Lord. Though your sins are like scarlet, they shall be as white as snow; though they are red as crimson, they shall be like wool.
>
> —Isa. 1:18

But he was pierced for our transgressions, he was crushed for our iniquities; the punishment that brought us peace was upon him, and by his wounds we are healed. We all, like sheep, have gone astray, each of us has turned to his own way; and the Lord has laid on him the iniquity of us all.

—Isa. 53:5–6

Here I am! I stand at the door and knock. If anyone hears my voice and opens the door, I will come in and eat with him, and he with me.

—Rev. 3:20

I especially liked the verses from Isaiah 53. I recalled the many times I had heard my own father preach from that text. Could it now possibly apply to my own life?

I heard myself cry out, "Lord God, please heal me! I promise to change my life. I'll change my attitude. I'll go to church … and mean it. I'll read my Bible and pray every day. I'll be a better father, a better husband, a better man. I'll do anything you ask. Please don't let me die!"

Promises made in the face of the threat of death by cancer.

Buried with the other materials in that cabinet was a booklet called *Scripture Keys for Kingdom Living*. I opened it and was surprised to see two handwritten notes, one penned by my father and one by my mother.

I read for the first time, "Dear Dave, as you study the Scriptures, may they be *life* to you. God bless you. Love, Dad" and "Great *treasures* lie within these pages, so dig deep and be blessed. Love you, Mom." The notes were dated February 16, 1992—five years earlier. The booklet had been casually tossed aside without a thought. I flipped through the contents page. I felt the rush of adrenaline as I reached a heading called "Healing." Oh, yeah! I was interested in that! In that section I found this verse: "Therefore I tell you, whatever you ask for in prayer, believe that you have received it, and it will be yours" (Mark 11:24).

How is that possible, when my prayers don't get any higher than the ceiling?

11

I went back to the contents page. The very next heading was "Hindrances Blocking Answers." I cautiously opened the booklet to the appropriate page and read, "Surely the arm of the Lord is not too short to save, nor his ear too dull to hear. Your iniquities have separated you from God; your sins have hidden his face from you, so that he will not hear" (Isa. 59:1–2).

Finally I realized my focus had to change from concern for my physical health to concern for my spiritual health. I quickly repeated my childhood prayer of salvation, "Dear God, please save me!"

Why should God save you? That nagging voice in my head again. But this time my theological education kicked in. God shouldn't save me. In fact, what I really deserved was his judgment. But didn't the doctrine of grace provide that he gave his only son Jesus to die so I could receive what I *didn't* deserve? Didn't the doctrine of mercy provide that God withholds from me the punishment I *do* deserve? What a concept! All I had to do was open the door and let him in. Redemption, reconciliation, and relationship could all be mine. I may have tried to forget about God—but God hadn't forgotten about me.

My prayer changed once again. "Jesus, forgive me of my sins. I want you to be the center of my life. I want to be ready to meet you when I die."

That's when I realized I had actually said the word *die* out loud. But somehow I was no longer afraid to die. No, I didn't *want* to die, but I was no longer afraid of the possibility. God had restored life to my dying soul.

Even so, while I was no longer anxious over my spiritual life, I still had problems with my physical life. I still had cancer. But now I knew how to pray. Now I had a personal relationship with the living Word.

Chapter Two

THE PERFECT ENDING

"Then you will call upon me and come and pray to me,
and I will listen to you. You will seek me and find me
when you seek me with all your heart. I will be found
by you, declares the Lord."
—Jeremiah 29:12-14 NLT

M Y WIFE, CAROLYN, is an extremely intuitive creature. Not only can she discern personality and character traits with frightening accuracy, but she can also predict actions before they happen and thoughts before they are verbalized. Yes, sometimes it's scary.

Carolyn accompanied me to every consultation with each member of our medical team. I was certain she could provide insight into the motives of the physicians who were assuring us their particular methods were right. Imagine my surprise when she remained strangely silent on the matter.

Almost two weeks had passed since our discussion of various treatment options. I finally understood her silence. The look of anguish in her beautiful blue eyes told me of her concern for my life and our future together. While she respected my need for active participation in the treatment process, she also needed to see tangible evidence of a move toward some attempt to eradicate the cancer in my body. "Please, David! Choose a treatment," she cried. "Do something—anything. Pick an option, and let's get this thing started."

I knew she was right. Having eliminated the mutilating surgical option, and despite my earlier proclamation to the contrary, we agreed that I would begin the chemotherapy-radiation regimen. With that decision our emotional roller-coaster catapulted us toward the top of another peak from which we would soon plunge into a loop of pain and despair. This time, however, we determined God's love would hold us tight during the ride. We were confident he could use any means he might choose to heal me—even chemotherapy and radiation.

We visited Dr. Seely to tell him of our decision. With renewed faith and trust, we enthusiastically reminded him that he had offered prayer as a treatment option. We told him of the many people praying for us all around the country. "In fact," I said, "we believe God has already begun to heal me. Perhaps we can avoid chemo and radiation."

"Really?" he responded. "Let's have a look."

As the doctor performed his now routine laryngoscopy, my wife held my hand tightly—prayerful he would not find the tumor.

"I'm sorry," the doctor said. "The tumor is still there; it's the same size, same shape, and same color. I think you should begin treatment as soon as possible."

Our hopes were shattered. We were plunged headlong into a pit of helplessness. What must God be thinking? Had he not heard our prayers? What was he planning to do with us?

PERFECT PEACE

In mid-November I was admitted to the oncology ward at Overlake Hospital. A catheter approximately twelve inches long was introduced into my right arm, running from mid-arm to the top of the bicep, with a saline solution drip attached. Once all preparations were complete, the oncologist arrived to write the prescription for cisplatin. I remained in the hospital overnight.

In the morning a pharmacist arrived with four vials of fluorouracil (5-FU). One of the vials, now attached to the catheter, began dripping its toxic content into my body. I was discharged from the hospital with three more vials of 5-FU and instructions for detaching the empty vial and replacing it with a new one until all the vials were empty.

I find it ironic that the side effects of chemotherapy are often minimized by those prescribing the drugs. They obviously have never voluntarily poisoned themselves. In fact, my oncologist suggested that I could even play golf with a bag of 5-FU attached to my arm. (But then, this is the same doctor who assured me that the drug-induced nausea could be alleviated with proper medication.) Buoyed by this false sense of security, I believed I was prepared for the potential side effects of the drugs: the nausea, the constipation, the esophageal burning and digestive-tract bloating.

I've never been more wrong.

By the third day these plagues began to manifest themselves in my body. I became indescribably ill. A heightened sense of smell soon encouraged nausea that could not be suppressed by any prescription medication.

Eating became a real challenge. My body desperately needed nourishment to heal itself from the damage caused by the drugs, but even when I was able to get the food down, my malfunctioning gastrointestinal system screamed in pain. The fiery sensation in my esophagus went unabated. The cramping in my lower digestive tract was like a giant hand squeezing my intestines. The constant ringing in my ears remains to this day. Day and night I struggled to find a comfortable position sitting or lying down. This plethora of painful problems made sleep a rarity, and the inability to achieve deep slumber only intensified the side effects.

With nowhere else to turn, I tried reading my Bible. Of course, I did not *feel* like reading the Bible, nor did I *feel* like praying. I was locked in the age-old struggle between what I knew and how I felt. I made choices based upon the pain I was feeling, rather than what I knew to be true. I knew God meant what he said in Hebrews 13:5: "Never will I leave you; never will I forsake you." So why did I feel so alone?

Here's irony for you. Whenever I read Scripture, prayed, or meditated on God's Word—even when I didn't *feel* like it—the pain and discomfort went unnoticed. Sometimes it wasn't there at all. Conversely, when I tried to watch television, think about the job I needed to get back to, or occupy my mind with something related to my physical plight, the pain seemed to worsen. I now understand what Isaiah the prophet meant when he wrote: "Thou wilt keep him in perfect peace, whose mind is stayed on thee" (Isa. 26:3 KJV).

As if the chemotherapy's side effects weren't enough, that first week was filled with infusion confusion.

After the third vial of 5-FU had found its way into my body, my wife and I tackled the awkward and challenging process of detaching the empty vial and attaching a full one. The vial itself was placed in my shirt pocket, since it needed to be higher than the catheter for proper flow; then the pocket was pinned closed to secure its poisonous content. After we attached the fourth vial, we noticed that it was leaking. Great! Now I had chemotherapy on my clothing and skin. This sent us into a tailspin toward panic. The 5-FU spilled onto Carolyn's hands when she grabbed a towel and began mopping up. "It's poison! It's poison!" I screamed.

Fortunately, she with the cooler head called the hospital oncology ward, only minutes from our home. The nurse on duty instructed her to bring me in immediately. Two nurses, gloved and gowned in toxic-waste cleanup garb, quickly removed my shirt and detached the leaking vial. One grabbed the towel Carolyn had used to sop up the drug and said, "This liquid is lethal. Anything that has been touched by the chemo must be destroyed." In my emotional stupor I thought, *Oh, no! They're going to cut off my wife's hands.* After some time a new vial arrived and we were sent home.

During the next two weeks, I continued to battle the chemotherapy side effects as my body tried to rid itself of its poisonous enemy. I was determined to rely upon God as my best source of hope for victory over the cancer invading not only my body but my entire life. After the last vial of 5-FU had dripped its way into my bloodstream, the catheter was removed. Having that apparatus out of my arm lifted my spirits more than I could have believed possible. Maybe I *could* get through this terrible ordeal.

PERFECT BLOOD COUNTS

On December 5, 1997, we visited the oncologist to have my white blood cell count checked. The cisplatin, he had told us, would likely destroy most of the cells necessary to the body's immune function.

The doctor reviewed the process for hospitalization and infusion of antibiotics to protect against various infections as we waited for the test report. His countenance changed as he reviewed the lab report. He glanced at us quizzically and looked at the report again. Then with astonishment in his voice he said, "Your blood count is perfectly normal. I don't understand."

We could barely contain our excitement. Had God answered our prayers and the prayers of so many others who had been interceding on our behalf? Yes, of course. This was just one of the many miracles God would use to increase our faith and trust in him—one step at a time.

A few days later we visited Dr. Seely for a follow-up to the first round of chemotherapy. The doctor was thrilled but surprised that my blood count was so normal. He took an unusually long time to perform another exam of my throat. Given our recent experience, we did not let anticipation raise our hopes.

Finally he said, "Wow. This really looks good."

OK. "What does 'really good' mean?" we asked with heart-pounding expectation.

"Well," he answered, "the tumor, originally the size of my thumb, is now no larger than the tip of my ballpoint pen."

What? Was he kidding? How was that possible after only one cycle of chemotherapy? I was scheduled for five more cycles of chemo and then radiation. The oncologist had been adamant that radiation would eradicate the cancer; chemo was only preparation for the radiation.

With excitement and relief in her voice, my wife said, "Doctor, we believe God has answered our prayers for healing."

"You might be right," he responded. "However—"

No! No! Not however, I thought. *Can't we just accept the fact that we've seen a miracle here?*

"However," the doctor continued, "if I were to biopsy that area, I'm certain we'd still find cancer. You need to complete the chemotherapy and radiation as scheduled."

We refused to let his suggestion dampen our spirits. We had seen a miracle. We were confident this was another answer to prayer—another means of building our faith, trust, and reliance upon God.

Notwithstanding, the thought of another course of chemotherapy sent chills to our very core. I had not fully recovered from the first course. My gastrointestinal system was not yet healed; my energy level seemed barely half of what it used to be. I wrestled with the decision to continue. Even in the face of these miraculous results, friends and relatives encouraged me to tough my way through another course. "After all, the doctor knows best," they claimed. In early December 1997 I admitted myself to Overlake Hospital to begin a second course of chemo.

Once again the side effects began to manifest themselves before the end of the first week. This time the 5-FU vials had to be changed in the late evening hours, which interrupted my sleep and created an undo hardship for my wife. After we completed the last vial change, I retired to bed. Approximately two hours later I felt something unusual in my arm. I turned on the light and saw a pool of blood surrounding the catheter site. I shouted out to my wife.

Once again she called the oncology ward, and in a matter of minutes we were on our way back to the hospital. As we made the short trip, I found myself in a free-fall of despair as that all-too-familiar emotional roller-coaster raced toward another deep, dark tunnel of hopelessness. I sobbed ... deep, heavy, can't-get-your-breath sobs. "If they have to take the catheter out of my arm, I will not let them replace it with a new one. I've had enough." All my wife could do was drive and pray.

Fortunately, the oncology team was able to clean up the problem without requiring a change of the catheter. We returned home to complete the chemotherapy infusion. After that last foul-smelling vial of chemo had found its way into my bloodstream, the catheter was removed from my arm and I began the slow process of recovery from the drugs.

PERFECT PRAYER

Not surprisingly, we began attending church on a regular basis. Additionally, my daily quiet time of prayer and Bible study had now become the most significant part of my day. I can tell you with certainty that the apostle James was right when he said, "Come near to God and he will come near to you" (James 4:8).

During one Sunday service, a men's 6 am breakfast and Bible study was announced for Wednesday. Now, I'd never been one for participating in Bible study, let alone one that started before most human beings were out of bed. Nevertheless, there was something in my heart urging me to attend. On Tuesday night I set the alarm for five A.M. Strangely, I was having the best night's sleep I'd had in weeks when the alarm sounded. My first reaction was to scold my wife for having set the alarm in the first place. Then I remembered—I'd set the alarm; Men's Bible study, six A.M.

Outside was a cold, rainy December morning. Certainly God would let me off the hook. After all, I was sick. Having rationalized my way out of the situation, I turned off the alarm and went back to sleep.

At five-fifteen I suddenly awoke. My right arm was completely without feeling. I don't mean it had fallen asleep or was tingling. The arm was lifeless. No feeling. I picked it up with my left hand. It felt as if I were picking up someone else's arm, except this one was cold and clammy. What was going on? Was God trying to tell me something?

Without hesitation I got out of bed and began preparing for the day. As I did, the feeling and use of my arm slowly returned. The message was clear: "Get up and go to the men's Bible study." I did.

The moment the pastor announced the morning's topic, "How to Pray with Victory," I knew why God wanted me there. Even though I was closer to God than I had been in my entire life, I continued to struggle with prayer: How should I pray? When should I pray? What should I pray?

That day the pastor defined prayer this way: "Prayer is not wrenching from an unwilling God something he is reluctant to release. It is, rather, opening the way for God to release what he's wanted to release, but hasn't, because no one prayed. Prayer is not overcoming God's reluctance; it is taking hold of his willingness." On that day, my prayer life changed forever. From that moment forward, I knew God wanted to answer my prayers—he was just waiting for me to pray.

PERFECT ODDS

On December 27, 1997, we returned to see Dr. Seely for follow-up to the second round of chemotherapy. We waited anxiously as he performed another examination of the tumor site. "Wow!" was all he could say. He could find no sign of the tumor. How was that possible? We knew the answer—God. Tears of joy and relief filled our eyes. Our fear and hopelessness changed to exhilaration and joy.

The doctor was understandably astonished. He had never seen such a response to chemotherapy after only two courses. He ordered an MRI, to be performed on December 31, as further confirmation of his findings. A review of the MRI was scheduled for January 2, 1998.

We immediately contacted everyone we knew to tell them God had answered their prayers. We had seen a miracle before our very eyes. Was this nightmare over? What would God do next? What purpose might be revealed for this experience?

On the day the MRI was to be performed, I said to my wife, "Let's make a deal. If the MRI comes back perfectly clear, I will not have further chemotherapy or any radiation." Reluctantly, she agreed. After the MRI procedure I rushed home with a copy of the film. We placed it up against the bathroom mirror along with the film from the MRI performed exactly two months earlier. Using our untrained eyes, we could find no evidence of tumor on the second film.

On January 2 we waited patiently in the examination room for Dr. Seely to give us his interpretation. When he arrived, he said, "I was just on the phone with the radiologist. He told me 'If I hadn't seen the first set of film, I'd tell you your patient is totally normal.'"

Another confirmation of our miracle!

"However—" he began.

Was he serious? Another *however*?

"However, there's a fifty-fifty chance that the cancer has spread to other areas of the body and we just can't detect it," he continued. "You need to complete the chemotherapy and radiation treatment regimen."

My mind raced with the realization that I was faced with more decisions that would affect the rest of my life. If I didn't have the chemo and radiation, would that prove to God that I truly believed he could completely heal me? On the other hand, if I did consent to the chemo and radiation, would that indicate to God that I really *didn't* believe he could completely heal me?

"Well, Doctor," I replied, "that means there's a fifty-fifty chance the cancer *hasn't* spread. I don't think I'm going to have any more chemotherapy, or any radiation."

"Really?" he said. "I think you may at least want to meet with the radiation oncologist for final closure of that chapter."

On January 11 I visited the radiation oncologist to review the results of the MRI. He compared the two sets of film and said, "This looks really good. To what do you attribute the change?"

"God has answered our prayers for healing," I replied.

"No, what are you *really* doing?"

Not knowing what he wanted to hear, I began to explain. In addition to the two courses of chemotherapy, I had completely changed my lifestyle; proper diet, regular exercise, periodic visits to the chiropractor, and the addition of natural supplements to assist my body's immune function to better fight the disease.

With a look of disdain and a condescending tone, he said, "Natural methods won't work. The only cure for this cancer is radiation. Without radiation the tumor will grow back within six to nine months to twice its original size. You'll be back here begging me to give you radiation. If you don't have the radiation, you will most surely die!"

I picked up the MRI film and my other belongings for a hasty departure from his office. I never saw him again.

I returned to see Dr. Seely each month in 1998, each quarter in 1999, twice in 2000, and once in 2001, for a complete examination of my head and neck. After each visit the doctor said, "You're better than you were the last time I saw you." MRIs were performed at six-month intervals—all completely clear. Could there be any doubt that God had performed a miracle?

PERFECT ENDING

This was the perfect ending to an otherwise tragic story. Why tragic? It took cancer to make me realize my need for an intimate relationship with God.

During my bout with the disease, a caring individual gave me Philip Yancey's book *Where Is God When It Hurts?* Yancey helped me stop asking why and start asking more forward-looking questions, For what purpose? and To what end?

I now saw more clearly what God had in mind by allowing me to go through the pain and misery I experienced in 1997. This was my personal wake-up call. God sounded it loud and clear with one purpose in mind; to bring me to a place of total reliance upon him. He reminded me that everything I had came from him. I was alive only because of him. Since 1997 I've recounted my experience hundreds of times to friends, relatives, co-workers, business associations, and church congregations, always giving God the glory for having performed a miracle in my body.

But I know what you're thinking—if God healed me of cancer in 1997, why was I receiving chemotherapy at the Seattle Cancer Treatment and Wellness Center in 2007? While there are many theories, there is only one answer.

Chapter Three

FEAR, THE GREAT MOTIVATOR

"So be truly glad!
There is wonderful joy ahead, even though it is necessary
for you to endure many trials for a while.
These trials are only to test your faith, to show
that it is strong and pure."
—1 Peter 1:6 NLT

HAVE YOU EVER been on an airplane during periods of unnerving turbulence? The one and only priority becomes a safe landing. Many people begin praying—in earnest. Maybe something like,

"Dear God, if I die today, my life would be a waste. I know I've ignored you most of the time but I promise you right now, if this plane makes it to the ground safely I'll change! Really! I'll keep all ten of the commandments. I'll be a better person. I'll begin a new life."

Later, after the plane has landed, a crash is no longer a possibility, and passengers are in the arms of loved ones, promises made to God are forgotten. Fear is replaced with baggage handling and transportation arrangements.

After the events of 9/11, statistics show that church attendance in America increased some seven-fold. People of all backgrounds and philosophies suddenly became believers in their need for divine protection from an unseen attacker.

Later, when the dust from the attack had settled, the rubble of the World Trade Center towers had been hauled away, and homeland security intensified its measures to make our boarders secure, church attendance in America again decreased to previous levels. Fear had been replaced with complacency and mediocrity.

Fear is a great motivator. Fear will change our priorities, our relationships, our attitudes, and our behaviors—at least temporarily. Fear will drive us to seek solace in places we would not otherwise seek it. Fear will encourage us to make choices we would not otherwise make. Fear will actually drive us to God.

After the fear of a dreadful disease had subsided, after the probability of death by cancer had seemingly ended, after the glow of my testimony had grown dim—so did the passion I felt toward my relationship with Jesus Christ. My humanness began to dictate my choices. I had become preoccupied with my resources, my relationships, my recreation, and even my religion. I had allowed the physiology of life—the way I was feeling emotionally, mentally, and physically, to influence my behavior.

Aleksander Solzhenitsyn, the Russian philosopher, said:

> More than half century ago, while I was still a child, I recall hearing a number of older people offer the following explanation for the great disasters that had befallen Russia: "Men have forgotten God. That's why all this has happened." Since then I have spent well-nigh fifty years working on the history of our revolution.... But if I were asked today to formulate as concisely as possible the main cause of the ruinous revolution that swallowed up some sixty million of our people, I could not put it more accurately than to repeat: "Men have forgotten God. That's why all this has happened."[2]

Had I forgotten what God had brought me through? That wasn't possible. Nevertheless, something had changed. I had tried to forget the many promises I made to God in exchange for my life. I was living at a speed that reflected an attitude toward godly behavior as one of option rather than one of obedience.

Fortunately, as I opened the Book looking for answers, I discovered I was not alone in my plight. Israel's King David wrote most of his psalms when he was in trouble—suffering through the consequences of his ungodly behavior. It was during these periods he talked most about God's love, mercy, loving-kindness, forgiveness, long-suffering, and healing.

When David was the most prosperous, the most revered, and the most independent, his passion for God's presence waned and his behavior changed. That's when God used the circumstances in David's life to remind him who was really in control. It was only after David had been through his own "valley of the shadow of death" that he was able to say to God, "You are the lifter of my head (Ps. 3:3); You are my high tower (Ps. 18:2); You are the redeemer of my soul (Ps. 19:14); You are the restorer of my health (Ps. 23:3); You are the rewarder of my faith (Ps. 31:23); You are the rebuilder of my hope (Ps. 16:9)."

WHAT ARE YOU DOING TO ME?

In September 2002 I visited Dr. Seely for my annual exam. He was stone-faced with amazement. The tumor had returned. "And it has returned with a vengeance," he said. "It looks to be larger than the one we found five years ago."

"How can that be?" I asked. This was the exam where cancer patients five years in remission are statistically pronounced clean.

My initial reaction was anger—at the doctor for giving me such bad news, at the thought of having to relive the horrible experience of cancer, at God for letting this happen to me. "Do you know how many people I've told that you healed me of cancer?" I said to God. (Of course he knew). "What am I supposed to tell them now? What are they going to think of me? What are they going to think of *you*? They'll never listen to me again. God, what are you doing to me?"

Most of all, I was angry at myself—angry for doing or not doing whatever it was I didn't do or should have done, angry for allowing my humanness to interfere with my relationship with God. Could he be using this situation to test our relationship? Possibly. Probably. Definitely. I was about to board that emotional roller-coaster for another death-defying ride.

Much as I had experienced in 1997, an MRI validated what the doctor had seen during his oral exam. Surgical biopsy performed the following day confirmed the doctor's suspicion of a recurrence of squamous cell carcinoma.

Both Dr. Seely and the oncologist agreed that the same chemo-therapy-radiation regimen was in order. "In fact," the oncologist said, "it worked so well the first time, we would be remiss not to try it again." *Go ahead. Poison me,* I thought. *I don't have the capacity or desire to deal with it. And yes, I am feeling quite sorry for myself.*

On November 13, 2002, I was admitted to the oncology ward at Overlake Medical Center where the treatment process began again: insertion of a midline catheter, overnight infusion of cisplatin, next-day discharge with a continuous forty-eight-hour infusion of 5-FU (this time with the aid of a portable pump, thanks to five years of technological improvement). It didn't take long for the side effects to begin. The nausea, burning, bloating, and cramping filled my head with memories of poisonous nightmares from the past. Why would I voluntarily do this to myself—again?

Upon removal of the catheter a week later, I noticed streaking red lines running from the catheter insertion point to the top of my shoulder and across my chest. Further examination confirmed thrombophlebitis—destruction of the local veins caused by the toxicity of the chemo drugs. Wonderful! Hearing loss, tinnitus, digestive tract issues, and now vein loss, all near-permanent side effects of chemotherapy.

I launched into intense research of alternative treatment methods. After only one course of chemo, I declined further infusions and visited the Northwest Natural Health Specialty Care Clinic in Seattle. Recommended lifestyle changes and a program of dietary supplements were immediately implemented into my daily routine.

I even had all the old amalgam fillings removed from my teeth. Would these changes help my body eradicate the tumor? Would any of it make a difference in my life? No one could say for certain. What could it hurt? Anything was better than chemotherapy!

Months passed. In February 2003 I visited Dr. Seely to determine whether my naturopathic lifestyle was having any significant effect. The result was the proverbial good news, bad news scenario. The tumor was still there (bad news), but it did not appear to have changed in size or shape (good news). The doctor ordered an MRI for comparison.

"A lobular soft tissue mass is centered in the right vallecula and right base of tongue" the report read. "This has shown interval decrease in size compared to the prior study." Great news!

With the results of this study in hand, I visited the oncologist on March 13 to discuss the reported decrease in tumor size. He was not impressed. In fact, he was insistent that the chemotherapy administered four months prior was responsible for the change. He was adamant that the chemo had prevented any spreading of the disease. He wanted credit for everything. He was puzzled, however, by the fact that my overall health was so good—no appetite or weight loss, no pain in the tumor area, no swallowing problems, no change in voice resonance, no breathing issues, no change in blood counts.

We discussed at length a plan for future treatment. Once again, he insisted that the continued infusion of cisplatin and 5-FU, followed by radiation, was the best and only method for a possible cure. How could he be so certain? According to statistics compiled by the University of North Carolina, 47 percent of males diagnosed with tongue-based squamous cell carcinoma died within five years irrespective of treatment—including traditional surgery, chemotherapy, or radiation.

Were there no other plausible treatment methods? My wife and I agonized through this quandary. Were we back where we started five years before? What exactly might God be trying to teach us? How could we continue to pray the same prayers when the answers we wanted didn't seem to come? What would we say to friends and relatives who had stood by us with their prayer and support? Should we just give up? Would life ever be normal again?

In October 2002 we had sold our primary residence and purchased two smaller homes—a condominium in Bellevue and a vacation home in Arizona. We planned to travel to Arizona in the spring of 2003 for a much-needed change of scenery. We informed the oncologist of our decision. He concurred that another physician in the Phoenix area could write a prescription for the chemotherapy. In March we met with Dr. Seely to inform him of our plans. He too concurred, with an additional offering: a former classmate of his was now performing head and neck surgery on cancer patients in Mesa, Arizona. Apparently the technological advances in this area provided some hope of tumor removal with less morbidity than that available five years before. We promised to contact him.

You Won't Survive

On April 18, 2003, we traveled to the Banner Desert Medical Center to discuss my case with the surgeon referred to us by Dr. Seely. He was short in stature, abrupt in speech, and confident in demeanor. After reviewing my files and performing his own examination, he insisted that he could successfully remove the tumor from my throat with only a "few" complications. While the actual surgery might have had fewer mutilating side effects, the potential for post surgical issues related to swallowing and breathing seemed not to have changed that much in five years.

Sensing my hesitation to immediately allow him to throw me on the table and cut out the tumor, the doctor became anxious and almost annoyed. Finally (I'm certain he was holding a scalpel behind his back), he looked at me and said, "The chemotherapy you've been given will never cure this disease. Radiation will not cure this disease. You need to let me remove that tumor from your throat. If you don't let me operate, it's likely you won't survive."

We were taken aback by his terse manner and lack of compassion. Sensing our irritation, he backpedaled and offered to provide names and numbers of patients happy to provide testimonials to his surgical successes. That was our last contact with him.

On April 21, 2003, we visited the Arizona Center for Hematology and Oncology to discuss the possibility for obtaining a prescription for cisplatin and 5-FU. The patient waiting area was filled with much-older men and women, all looking drawn, sickly, and desperate. As I surveyed the scene, I thought, *I don't belong here!* I should have trusted my instincts and left. I didn't.

Finally, the receptionist called my name. After another long wait in an examination room, we were introduced to the oncologist reviewing my case. He was short in stature, abrupt in speech, and confident in demeanor. (Same song, different verse.)

Without hesitation he said, "I've been looking through your files and must tell you that you were given the wrong chemotherapy drugs during your treatment in Washington." This was not what we expected to hear. How many more mixed messages and uncertainty from the medical community could we handle? Had he not read the results of the chemotherapy regimen administered in 1997?

The doctor proceeded to list the drugs he would prescribe in combination with radiation over the next several weeks—and possibly months. My wife and I exchanged glances that asked, Now what do we do?

We assured the doctor our sole purpose in seeing him was to obtain the same prescription I had used before. With that, he became excited. He stood up from his chair and said, "I've handled hundreds of cases like yours. I know what works and I know what doesn't work against squamous cell carcinoma. If you don't accept the regimen I prescribe, you will die!"

I grabbed my medical records and we left, never to return.

Whom were we supposed to believe? Here were two different physicians from two different backgrounds and disciplines each telling us that his recommendation for treatment was the only one that might save my life. Fortunately, attempts to frighten me into action did not work; I would not be intimidated by the fear factor. I would not be cornered into believing that one particular discipline had the answer—particularly when members of the same discipline did not agree.

Help My Unbelief

We were now more confused than at any other moment in our battle with cancer. Worse, we no longer had any meaningful direction for treatment. The emotional pain returned with a furor. "Dear God, where are you?" I prayed. In my heart I really didn't expect him to answer. I began to doubt that he had ever been involved in my situation. At the same time I was overcome with guilt for even thinking that.

As the son of a God-fearing, well-meaning, Pentecostal preacher, I had been raised to believe that those who suffer should always smile, that death should always be celebrated and never grieved, that only heretics ask questions like, "If God is so good, why is my life so bad?" In fact, for many of the Christians I knew, doubt was just a spiritually correct way of describing unbelief.

Could that be true? Was my relationship with God in jeopardy simply because I asked questions about my circumstances? Would God turn his back on me simply because I needed to understand why I had to suffer?

A few days later I was describing to some friends our visit with the death-predicting oncologist and the survival-questioning surgeon. I explained my reaction, my mental confusion, and my concern about whether God was still interested in me. In response, our friends gave us a cassette tape of a sermon delivered by one of their associate pastors. The moment I began listening to the tape, I knew God was still involved in my circumstances. He knew the doubt I was experiencing; he heard the questions I was asking.

The sermon was centered on Jesus' disciple Thomas—doubting Thomas as he's come to be known. The pastor described my spiritual quandary with extrasensory precision. Using Thomas as an example, he offered the idea that questions can actually be a quest for faith, that honest doubt is a step forward in faith, and that faith can be strengthened by sincere investigation.

Maybe I wasn't doomed after all! I was really like the father in Luke 9, whose son was being harassed by a demon. The father brought the boy to Jesus and said, "Lord, if you can help me—" Jesus stopped him and said, "*If* I can help you? All things are possible to those who believe!" Then this hurting, searching father said, "Lord, I believe. Help my unbelief."

That was me. Keep in mind, I never doubted my faith in Jesus Christ; I never doubted the power of his blood; I never doubted the truth of his resurrection. I knew God was capable. I just didn't know if I could muster enough faith to believe that God still cared about me after I'd disappointed him. It's easy to doubt when you experience an unexpected setback, when you pray for one thing and the opposite happens, when you lose a friend, a job, a relationship, or health.

So is doubt a sign of weakness or instability? Is doubt sinful? The pastor suggested in his sermon that some great heroes of the Bible had their seasons of doubt about God and his involvement in their lives:

From the searching questions of Job: "Though I cry, 'I've been wronged!' I get no response; though I call for help, there is no justice. He has blocked my way so I cannot pass; he has shrouded my paths in darkness. He has stripped me of my honor and removed the crown from my head. He tears me down on every side till I am gone; He uproots my hope like a tree" (Job 19:7–10).

To the puzzled anxiety of David: "Why, O Lord, do you stand far off? Why do you hide yourself in times of trouble?" (Psa. 10:1).

To the painful cries of Jeremiah: "He has walled me in so I cannot escape; he has weighed me down with chains. Even when I call out or cry for help, he shuts out my prayer" (Lam. 3:7–8).

Wow! I was in pretty good company. Comforting, but what do I do now?

GUESS WHO MOVED

I hit the Internet with renewed fervor searching for something—anything—that might offer hope for combating the tumor in my throat. Finally, I happened upon a site describing a treatment that offered individualized, integrative cancer care and immune support, along with natural therapies that empower the patient to attack the cancer, boost the immune system, reduce the side effects, and support the whole—body, mind, and spirit—throughout treatment and beyond. The Cancer Treatment and Wellness Centers of America (CTWC) had been treating cancer patients throughout the country with above-average results. Had I found an approach to cancer treatment that might actually be the correct one?

It was certainly refreshing to find an organization with a mission for treating the patient and not just the disease. Upon our return to Washington in early May 2003, I contacted the Seattle facility of the CTWC and made an appointment for evaluation. I found the physicians and other team members to be some of the most caring and compassionate people we had encountered.

The oncologist assigned to my case for a preliminary examination reviewed my medical files. He was amazed at my physical health. "You don't look like a cancer patient," he said. "No appetite or weight loss? No tumor pain? No swallowing or speech problems?"

"None of the above."

"According to your MRI, the tumor does not appear to have spread. That's not typical of squamous cell carcinoma. How do you explain that?"

I quickly told him that God had answered the prayers of literally hundreds, and possibly thousands, of people. "It is God who must receive the credit."

"You might be right. There does not appear to be any other plausible explanation. However, there is a still a tumor growing in your throat, and pathology confirms it to be cancer. We need to discuss a form of treatment."

The doctor recommended a regimen of chemotherapy infusions using four drugs to be administered each week for a period of twelve weeks. Believing I may have found the answer, I began the treatment process. Despite this fractionated-dosage concept,

I became extremely disillusioned as the cumulative effects of the poisons took their toll on my body.

I lasted through the fifth week. I was only sick, uncomfortable, and in pain when I was being treated, I reasoned. Otherwise I had no physical problems related to the unyielding tumor in my throat. I was reasonably healthy. I had plenty of energy and no pain. Right or wrong, I discontinued treatment. My decision was in no way a reflection of the care and support I had received from the team at SCTWC. I simply could no longer voluntarily poison myself.

But I was ready to try anything, no matter how extreme, that might provide an eradication of the tumor without the side effects associated with chemotherapy. I needed help. *Help!* I found myself reciting that one-word prayer over and over again. The questions remained. Did God hear me? Should I expect an answer? Why did he seem so distant?

During one Sunday morning church service in June, the worship leader asked, "If God seems far away, guess who moved?" That question found its mark in the very center of my heart. No wonder I felt as though God were ignoring me. No wonder I couldn't find answers or hear him anymore—I was no longer within earshot. The noise of my life was drowning out the still, small voice of his Holy Spirit.

My own behavior had created a gap in the close fellowship I had once enjoyed with a heavenly Father. I examined my life yet again. I realized that God had always been with me, despite my move away from him. How else could I explain my excellent health or that the tumor itself remained isolated and indolent? So what exactly might be God's purpose for allowing me to go through this horrifying experience again? What was the lesson he wanted me to learn, and would I apply it to my life?

RANDOM ACTS OF DESPERATION

With a renewed sense of confidence and hope, I continued my research. I was determined to find a pain-free method of treatment. By mid-July I had become so anxious that I pursued several testimonials praising the results of something called vibratory energy medicine. "This medicine is based upon the premise that each disease has one or more specific polarity reversal rates per second that kill it. A vibration energy device is used to produce mechanical vibrations in the patient of the same frequency as the polarity reversal rate."

Huh?

"It also produces vibrations equal to odd multiples of the polarity reversal rate (frequency). If the main frequency of vibration, or one of the odd multiples, equals or is close enough to one of the vibration frequencies that kill the disease, then the disease can be killed by this method."

OK.

Opponents of such radical alternative care called this treatment method quackery. However, a friend with prostate cancer said he had tried the treatment and truly believed it had helped him. He gave me contact information, and for no other reason than sheer desperation I pursued this painless alternative with all haste.

Eight hundred dollars and two 180-mile round trips later, the tumor had not changed in any material respect; so much for random acts of desperation.

The feelings of emptiness and helplessness were once again closing in. I was now satisfied to place everything in God's hands. I had burned through all my resources. I *had* to depend upon him to deal with my problem. Whatever he wanted to do with me would be acceptable. I was too exhausted to deal with the situation any longer. Anything he demanded, I would promise.

Chapter Four

MEET MY NEW BEST
FRIEND

"The Lord is kind and merciful, slow to get angry,
full of unfailing love."
—Psalm 145:8 NLT

ONE AFTERNOON IN late July 2003, as my wife stood in the grocery store check-out line near the magazine rack, her gaze fell on the most recent issue of *Prevention*. For no conscious reason she picked it up and placed it with her other items.

Leafing through the magazine later that week, she spotted a barely noticeable information box extolling the recent success of a cancer treatment called photodynamic therapy. She quickly called the article to my attention.

"Oh, that," I grunted.

Photodynamic therapy (PDT) was one of the many cutting-edge cancer treatments I had investigated in 1997. The treatment process begins with the injection of a light-activated drug called Photofrin (*porfimer sodium*) that passes through normal cells but is absorbed by cancer cells. After seventy-two hours the cancer cells are exposed to a special laser light. The light, in combination with the drug, produces a miniature explosion, and the cancer is effectively burned up—ablated.

As part of my research, I had sent all my medical files to a physician in the Midwest, who was pioneering the use of PDT as a treatment for certain esophageal cancers. Upon review of my case, he had responded that given the location of the tumor, I was not a candidate for PDT. With that in mind I dismissed my wife's suggestion to read *Prevention*'s piece on the subject.

"Technology has changed in six years" she insisted. She read, "Dr. Paul Castellanos at the University of Maryland Medical Center in Baltimore is leading the way in the use of PDT for head and neck cancer patients." Persistent (as wives can be), she made me promise that I would call this Castellanos fellow.

I took the magazine to my office and set it aside. A few days later I spied it peeking at me from under a stack of other materials and decided I had nothing to lose by making a toll-free call to Dr. Castellanos's clinic. I described my case to the assistant who answered the phone. "I'm positive the doctor would like to talk to you," she said. "Can I have him call you tomorrow?"

Given my recent experience with certain members of the medical profession, I didn't believe I could count on anything. I was never more delighted to be wrong. The next day Dr. Castellanos called and talked with me for more than twenty minutes. His tone was compassionate without being condescending. He listened to my plight with a caring attitude and a desire to become involved in my treatment. His questions extended beyond my medical history to my emotional and mental state—all from three thousand miles away.

At his request I forwarded my complete medical history. Upon receipt of the documents, he called again to say he would like to discuss in more detail the possibility of treatment. He asked if I would call him later that evening at his residence. "It will have to be around nine-thirty eastern time," he said. "That will give us the opportunity for family prayer time and getting our children into bed."

Did he say prayer time? And what kind of physician offers to speak with a prospective patient from his own home at nine-thirty at night? I had to know more about him. I would definitely make that call.

My first question, following our exchange of greeting, was, "Doctor, in our earlier conversation you mentioned a family prayer time. Would you be willing to share a little more about that?"

"Absolutely," he answered. "The most important thing we do every day is to involve our children in the building of our family with God as its foundation."

I could barely contain my excitement. As we shared, I assured the doctor that we too believed God to be the foundation for life and dealing with the problems that come with it. Immediately we created a bond that would extend far beyond the usual doctor-patient relationship.

We discussed my case. He was fascinated by my story. Having reviewed the details of my most recent exam and MRI, he said, "I'm sorry. Given the depth of the tumor, it doesn't appear you are a candidate for PDT. The drug currently available for the procedure (Photofrin) will not penetrate deep enough. But have you considered transoral laser microsurgery?" He described the procedure as a newly developed surgical alternative to the mutilating scalpel resection offered me in 1997. A cutting laser would be used to remove the tumor one small piece at a time via an oral cavity; in my case, the mouth. (The surgery has far less morbidity than the traditional surgical process.) Dr. Castellanos was one of only a handful of head and neck surgeons regularly performing transoral laser microsurgery (TOLMS), a relatively new procedure in the United States. We concluded our discussion with my promise that I would research TOLMS and keep him posted on any decision for treatment.

Over the next two months, I spent hours researching TOLMS. In August I located a surgeon at the Harborview Medical Center in Seattle who was using the treatment in his practice. I quickly made an appointment to discuss my interest in using this new surgical technique without having to travel to the other side of the country.

When the doctor noted the location and size of the tumor, he became noticeably quiet. Curious about his reticence, I began to ask questions related to his experience with TOLMS. One question I asked was how many laser resections he had performed to remove head and neck cancers.

He hesitated. "Well, less than five."

Less than five? That could mean one! The doctor seemed relieved when I thanked him for his time and said I would investigate further before making a decision.

Great is your Faithfulness

My work began to suffer as I spent more and more time away from my job for research and multiple sessions with medical professionals. My strength and endurance were diminished and my cognitive ability affected. Something had to give.

On September 3 I faxed Dr. Castellanos the reports and film of an MRI performed in August 2003. Like those who had reviewed my case before him, the doctor was astonished that after almost a year since recurrence, the tumor in my throat had remained localized and stabilized. He found it difficult to believe that the cancer had not spread into my lymph system. He asked me the same questions others had asked about my physical condition. No weight or appetite loss? No pain at the tumor site? No swallowing or breathing or voice problems? No coughing up blood?

Why did I not display any of the usual symptoms associated with this type of cancer? Could it be that the chemotherapy had kept the disease in check? Were the changes in my diet and added supplements having a greater-than-anticipated impact? Maybe. But why is it that we are so willing and so quick (and even anxious) to attribute the positive results of questionable circumstances to human intervention? We had prayed, hadn't we? Why wouldn't we expect God to answer our prayers? Isn't that what we call faith? Why would I have ever doubted God? (Oops. Had I actually said that out loud?)

God was using my own words to teach me a valuable lesson. I finally realized that he had not slapped me around just because I had asked questions about my circumstances. He had not excommunicated me from our relationship because I doubted his concern. He had not abandoned me when I failed the test of faith. Rather, he allowed me to vent my anger, frustration, and disappointment; then he lovingly, mercifully, and compassionately responded to my doubt.

As it was with the disciple Thomas, God was simply saying, "It's OK. You can stop doubting now. Here is all the evidence you need that I am still an active participant in your life." And like Thomas, I fell to my knees and cried, "My Lord and my God."

I had finally taken the advice of the young pastor I heard on that cassette tape given to me by friends. I had to admit that I do, in fact, have occasion to doubt. I simply had to acknowledge the evidence God provided. In my case, it was a medical condition that did not act normally, a cancer that should have—but had not—spread to other parts of my body, a tumor that remained isolated and accessible, a physical capacity not yet inhibited by this dreadful disease.

Remember those Bible heroes who had their questions and doubts about God's participation in their lives? Each one of them, because they *wanted* to believe, actually found the way:

Job, who doubted big time, finally got it together and said, "I know that my Redeemer lives, and that in the end he will stand upon the earth. And after my skin has been destroyed, yet in my flesh I will see God" (Job 19:25–26).

David, who earlier accused God of hiding in times of trouble, said, "God is our refuge and strength, an ever-present help in trouble" (Psa. 46:1).

Jeremiah, who struggled with what he thought was God's avoidance said, "Because of the Lord's great love we are not consumed, for his compassions never fail. They are new every morning; great is your faithfulness" (Lam. 3:22–23).

You Need Surgery Now!

The summer months passed quickly. In early October we traveled to our vacation home in Arizona to escape the damp, dark weather pattern of the Seattle area. After two weeks I returned alone to Seattle to resume work.

During this period I continued to exchange e-mails with Dr. Castellanos concerning treatment. He suggested that I travel to Baltimore for an evaluation of TOLMS as a treatment. I suggested that I could make the trip in early January 2004. This gave the doctor cause for concern. He was not keen on doing "nothing" for an extended period of time, even though the disease had not spread at this point. I agreed to travel from Seattle to Baltimore in November. That meant, however, I would be making the trip without my wife.

I arrived on November 10, 2003. Dr. Castellanos's staff had made arrangements for me to stay in a housing facility specifically maintained for hospital patients and their families. The facility, interestingly enough, was located in Baltimore's highest drug-trafficking area. The next morning I decided to take a cab to the University of Maryland campus for my appointment with Dr. Castellanos. The nearest taxi stand was at the Greyhound bus depot several blocks away. On my way, I realized what an ethnic minority I was in the area. Almost embarrassed by my fear, I began to pray, "Lord, please protect me from bodily harm!"

I found a cab and got in the back seat, and that's when I heard the words and music of the song "My Tribute" by Andre Crouch coming from the speakers at the back of the vehicle: "To God be the glory, for the things he has done!" Suddenly, all the anxiety and fear drained from my body. One more time God proved his presence in my life. One more time he proved his desire to be an active participant in my circumstances.

Dr. Castellanos was short in stature. *Oh, boy!* However, his smile was warm. His demeanor was inviting. I extended my hand in greeting. Instead, he embraced me like a brother he hadn't seen in some time. Immediately, Paul Castellanos appeared seven feet tall.

He performed a thorough exam using the latest technology and video equipment. The tumor was evident and appeared accessible. After the exam, the doctor confirmed again that photodynamic therapy was not an option. In fact, given the size of the tumor and the stage of the disease, the doctor said, "We need to schedule surgery sooner than later. Can you extend your trip a few days?"

This had not been part of my travel plans. I was hoping to schedule any treatment for a later date, when my wife could be with me. However, I felt a peace about the doctor's recommendation and agreed to transoral laser microsurgery scheduled for November 14, 2003.

I passed the pre-op physical examination with flying colors. No symptoms of cancer noted. I was still in excellent health. Nevertheless, I had a malignant tumor growing in my throat, about to be removed using a relatively new surgical procedure performed by a man I had met only one day before. Now, *that's* faith!

The night before surgery, I struggled to sleep. I replayed the events of the past several years, trying to make sense of what God was trying to teach me. I came to realize that every test in life has two things in common: First, it always involves a choice, and second, the test is always "open book." Sadly, we often exhaust our resources in search of the right answers and never open the book. I determined this would not be the case.

I opened the Book and read from Psalm 103: "The Lord is compassionate and merciful, slow to get angry and filled with unfailing love. He will not constantly accuse us, nor remain angry forever.... The Lord is like a father to his children, tender and compassionate to those who fear him. For he knows how weak we are; he remembers we are only dust. Our days on earth are like grass; like wildflowers, we bloom and die. The wind blows, and we are gone—as though we had never been here" (vv. 8–9, 13–16 NLT).

Once more God would prove his love and faithfulness. Once more I was gripped with shame for having ever doubted him. Once more he would provide a powerful lesson for my life.

In the early morning of November 14, the doctor visited me in the pre-op ward to discuss the specifics of surgery. He introduced me to the anesthesiologist and provided details concerning postoperative care. He confirmed that my stay in Baltimore would have to be extended by at least a week to ensure against any post-op issues.

Once all preparations had been made, I was wheeled into an elaborate operating theater. Just before they administered the anesthesia, I asked Dr. Castellanos if I could pray. He took my hand and said, "Absolutely! You'll find several believers right here in the room with you."

I prayed aloud. I thanked God for having kept the tumor accessible. I thanked him that the cancer had not spread to other parts of my body, for revealing himself to me through his Word, and for the availability of the medical resources about to be provided. I asked him to guide the doctor's hand and give him wisdom to make the best decisions possible. I asked him to fill the room with his presence. I asked all of this in the name of his Son, Jesus.

Suddenly, a large African-American gentleman, dressed in surgical garb, said with a deep, loud voice, "Amen!" I knew I was in good hands. I knew that before he placed his hands upon me, my new friend Paul Castellanos had placed himself in God's hands.

When I awoke in recovery, more than twelve hours had passed. The surgery had taken almost ten hours. The tumor had been rooted deeper than the MRI indicated, producing unanticipated problems. Dr. Castellanos later told me that he had left the operating room twice. The first time he left to pray. He prayed for me and he prayed for himself. He asked God to protect me and to give him wisdom as he continued the surgery. When he left the second time, the rest of the surgical team was puzzled and wondered what was happening.

"I wasn't certain I could continue with the operation," the doctor told me. "The tumor had rooted itself deeply into sub-mucosal tissues and was much larger than it had appeared on the MRI. I didn't want to call your wife some three thousand miles away and ask her to make a decision by telephone. After praying again, I was convinced this was your last best hope for being rid of the tumor. I had to continue. I chased that thing around until I was sure I got it all."

ISN'T GOD GOOD?

After two days in intensive care and another day and a half in the hospital, I was discharged on a cold, rainy Baltimore afternoon. With a couple of prescriptions for pain medication, I was dismayed to find that the hospital pharmacy had closed only minutes before. I would have to locate an off-site pharmacy as well as transportation to get there.

I used the lobby telephone to call a taxi. To be certain I got my ride, I waited on the cement island under the hospital entrance portico. This wouldn't have been so bad except for the rainy, windy weather, my extremely weakened condition, and the unbelievably large volume of people trying to get in and out of the medical complex. Thirty minutes went by; no cab. I went back into the lobby and called the company dispatcher again. No answer. I went back to my spot under the portico. Now forty-five minutes had passed. I was feeling like I might pass out. Holding my head in my hands, I finally prayed. *Help!*

That one heartfelt word was all I needed. God heard me. Within seconds I saw a cab drive up to the curb, but not from the company I had called. No one got in. The driver pulled away but returned a few moments later. Once again, no passengers approached the cab. Seeing my opportunity, I knocked on the window and asked if the cab was available. Its elderly African-American driver waved me in.

I explained my dilemma and the need for a stop at a pharmacy before going to my hotel. "No problem," he said. "There's one only a mile or so away." As we drove toward the exit, the driver asked, "What were you in for?" Without thinking, I launched into an abridged version of my situation; the cancer, the tumor, the surgery, and how God had answered all of my prayers throughout this trying ordeal.

Without hesitation the driver turned and said, "Isn't God good!" On the short trip from the pharmacy to my hotel, we exchanged verses from the Book and talked of God's faithfulness and loving-kindness. I thanked him over and over again for being there at the right time. Did God know what I needed and when I needed it? Of course he did. He was proving to me yet again how much I could trust him; how much he loved and cared about me.

As I paid the driver, he said, "You know, it's funny. My dispatcher sent me to the hospital to pick up a female passenger. Never once did anyone approach my cab. So when you knocked on the window, I figured I might as well take the fare."

I've told that story countless times. After each telling, at least one person suggests that the cab driver might have been an angel sent by God. I don't know whether he was an angel—but I know he was sent by God.

I spent the next three days slowly recovering from surgery. The pieces of tumor cut from my throat had been sent to the medical center's pathology laboratory and fit together like a puzzle. The mass was then used to determine the successful removal of the malignancy.

A couple of days later, the doctor called with the results. "The margins are clear. It appears we were able to successfully remove the tumor."

I was overcome with joy. I offered my thanks and praise to God over and over again for performing yet another miracle in my body. During my follow-up exam, I conveyed my sentiments to Dr. Castellanos. Even though he wanted to believe a miracle had taken place, his medical discipline made him cautious. He asked me to return to Baltimore in February for a surgical biopsy to ensure the absence of any residual tumor. I agreed.

I ordered a car from Davis Limousine Service to transport me to the airport. As it happened, the car was driven by the owner of the company himself. On the drive to the airport, we engaged in casual conversation about things like differences in East Coast and West Coast living, families, sports, and the latest political battles.

I was not aware at the time what God had planned for our driver-passenger relationship.

Hey! My Name is Greg

I spent the next several months recovering from surgery. It was almost a year before I returned to work full-time. In December 2003 and again in January 2004, I visited Dr. Seely for further examinations. He was amazed at the surgical results and noted nothing more than an asymmetry in my throat.

I traveled to Baltimore via Washington, D.C. in February 2004 for biopsy surgery. I made arrangements with Davis Limousine Service for round-trip transportation between Baltimore and Dulles International Airport. Once again, none other than the company's owner drove the car. For the second time, our conversation was light and casual. We talked about the historical sites around Washington DC, the best places to eat in Baltimore, the Orioles and Mariners, the Ravens and the Seahawks.

Mr. Davis dropped me at the Marriott, and I called Dr. Castellanos to alert him of my arrival. The following day he performed his own exam in preparation for the biopsy. Surgery was performed the next day on an outpatient basis, and I was discharged to my hotel later the same day.

Friday morning, the day after surgery, the doctor called to check on me and asked if I would like to attend a weekend church retreat with him and his wife. Apparently, one participant had canceled, leaving an open spot. The retreat included an overnight stay on Friday and conference activities on Saturday. Since my return flight to Seattle wasn't until Sunday afternoon, I had no reason to refuse.

That afternoon Dr. Castellanos picked me up at my hotel and shuttled me to his home in nearby Hanover. His four beautiful children joyously greeted us. I was finally able to put faces to the rest of the family I had learned so much about. We packed up the car, said good-bye to the children, and made the hour-long trip to the retreat. The Friday-evening activities included food, greetings, music, worship, and an inspirational teaching by the guest speaker. Nothing I had not expected. The big surprise came when we were given our dormitory assignments. Since I was a single and all the rooms were doubles, I would be spending the night (in very close quarters) with a perfect stranger.

I was first to arrive at the room and found two very small twin beds and a bathroom just large enough to turn around in. No radio, no television, no toiletries, no hair dryer, no bathrobe, no mini-bar. The only light was a small lamp on a very small table between the very small beds.

Now, I'm a reasonable person. I can tolerate a lot of inconvenience. But I had experienced surgery less than twenty-four hours earlier and was using sizeable quantities of medication to suppress the postoperative pain. My mood was not the best, and I was not certain how much I could endure on top of my physical condition. I had begun to unpack when the door burst open and in walked my roommate—large, bald, tattooed, and pierced. What had I gotten myself into? Was this guy at the wrong retreat?

"Hey," he said, "my name is Greg."

"Hi," I squeaked, "my name is David. You know, like David and Goliath?"

"Great," he grunted, surveying the room. Eyeing the bed closest to the door, he declared, "I'll take that one."

"You got it, Greg!" I quickly responded. "I'm easy." *And I don't want to do anything that might irritate you!*

"No TV?" he snarled. "I guess that means we'll have to talk."

Oh, boy.

As it turned out, Greg was the retreat's worship leader (that explained the guitar case he was carrying). I felt relieved until he unpacked a facemask that looked like something from *Silence of the Lambs.*

"I hope this doesn't bother you," he said, holding up the mask. "I suffer from sleep apnea and have to wear this thing to get me through the night. I hook it up to this pump and it provides just the right amount of air into the mask." When he turned it on later that night, the pump sounded like the labored breathing of Darth Vader.

Terrific, I thought. *Now I know who won't be sleeping tonight.*

As he settled in, Greg asked me how I came to be a retreat participant. I explained my relationship with Dr. Castellanos and his invitation to join him and his wife for the weekend. Before long, I was telling him my whole story. Not only because there was no TV, but also because Greg had suggested that's what we'd do. My frustration and anxiety subsided. I described how God had brought me out of a life of sin and how he had performed miracle upon miracle in my life and in my body.

Greg listened intently. After several minutes, tears began to fill his eyes, and his large shoulders began to shudder. I was ashamed at having allowed myself to make assumptions about this sensitive individual based on his physical appearance.

Through tears and sobs Greg told me his own story of deliverance from drugs, alcohol, and other debilitating habits. He had been a member of a hard-rock band and had experienced a side of life with which I was not familiar. However, we did have one thing in common: God had used near tragic circumstances to get our attention and set us free from our independence. Greg was now using his talent to serve the God who had graciously saved his life.

After our brief time together, Greg and I agreed we were not just roommates but brothers in Christ—"soul" mates—each with a desire to have our attitudes and behaviors testify that our lives were possessed by God and not the stuff the world used to define us. God had indeed orchestrated our room assignments. After all, God's timing is perfect, and he doesn't waste anything. Just ask him.

Hey, Buddy!

The conference activities continued Saturday morning with breakfast, group worship time, and study time facilitated by the guest speaker. During the lunch break, Dr. Castellanos and I were once again reviewing the facts of my medical situation. "I've treated hundreds of cases of head and neck cancers," he said, "and never have I seen anything like yours. Most patients with stage IV squamous cell carcinoma seldom recover completely, particularly since the nature of this cancer is to spread quickly." We agreed that the only explanation was God's involvement in my case, sparing me for reasons yet to be revealed.

We reminisced about how our relationship had evolved from doctor and patient to close friends. Paul (I no longer called him Dr. Castellanos) remarked, "During my years as a medical professional, I've had many friends who have become my patients. Seldom has a patient become a close friend."

"Well, you know why that is, don't you, Paul?" I replied. "We have a bond that transcends mere friendship. We have a bond in Jesus Christ." To this day our relationship has only become stronger. As we would later discover, God brought us together for purposes far more important than medical treatment.

Later that evening we returned to Paul's home, where he and his wife invited me to spend the night. Before retiring, I was privileged to participate in the family's prayer time. I watched in awe as each child in turn—starting with the youngest—was given the opportunity to offer thanks to God and lift petitions for his grace and mercy. Nicholas, Maria, Lucas, and Stephen each took turns. When it was eleven-year-old Stephen's turn, I was astonished by his mature, thoughtful, articulate, and heartfelt prayer, a testament to the example and instruction provided by his parents. In the wake of his entreaty, I struggled to form proper sentences when it came my turn to offer thanksgiving for all God had done for me.

On Sunday I was delighted to attend church with the family. Afterward, we stopped at KFC and picked up a chicken dinner to enjoy around the family's table.

Toward the end of the meal and after the children had been dismissed, Paul's beeper sounded. He noted the number and dialed his cell phone. I heard bits and pieces of his end of the conversation: "Who is the head nurse on duty?" "What are his vital signs?" "Has the family been notified?"

When the conversation was over, Paul said, "Kids, come here. We need to pray." Paul's wife, Katherine, and all four children came bounding without hesitation from their various places in the house and stood around their father. With tears filling his eyes, he put his arms around them and began to pray. He prayed for a patient who was now on his deathbed. He prayed for the patient's family. He asked God for wisdom and guidance in his participation in their lives. He thanked God for his mercy and love.

After concluding his prayer, he looked at me and said, "David, that was about a man who had the same type of tumor you have. Cancer was discovered in his throat not more than eighteen months ago and has already spread to other parts of his body. Now he is dying, and there is nothing more I can do for him but pray."

Was there a message for me in this situation? Was there a reason I was privy to this scene? Had God placed me there for a specific purpose? Absolutely! This was one more confirmation that God had worked yet another miracle in my life, and only he was to get the credit for it.

CONVERSATIONS WITH A CASUAL OBSERVER

Since I would not be traveling to the airport from my hotel, I had called the limo service and left a message that I would need a pickup in Hanover instead. The car arrived at the appointed time, driven again by its owner. I said my good-byes to the Castellanos family, and we started toward the airport. As we pulled away, Mr. Davis asked, "Who were those people? Do you have relatives here?" I explained that this was the home of the physician who had performed my surgery.

"What?" he exclaimed. "Doctors don't invite their patients to stay overnight with them." He was anxious for details. During the forty-five minute ride to Dulles, I shared my experience with this curious onlooker. I tried providing only bits and pieces, but he wasn't satisfied. The more I shared, the more questions he asked. I finally told him an abridged version of my story, starting from October 1997.

As I concluded with a description of the incident that had taken place at the Castellanos residence only minutes before I left, tears filled his eyes. I saw him glance at me in the rearview mirror as he told me about the struggle he was having with his teenage son, how he and his wife were attempting to raise their children in a godly manner, and the difficulties confronting them in their efforts. He poured out his heart's desire to be a godly man and thanked me over and over for my willingness to share my experience.

I asked if I could read a passage of Scripture that had become my testimony these past seven years. With his consent I read from Psalm 116 in *The Living Bible* paraphrase: "I love the Lord because he hears my prayers and answers them. Death stared me in the face—I was frightened and sad. Then I cried, 'Lord save me!' How kind he is! How good he is! So merciful this God of ours! He has saved me from death, my eyes from tears, my feet from stumbling. I shall live! Yes, in his presence—here on earth! In my discouragement I thought, 'They are lying when they say I will recover.' But now what can I offer Jehovah for all he has done for me?"

As we approached the airport entrance, I asked if I could pray with him. With tears streaming down his face, he nodded his head. I leaned forward and placed my hand upon his right shoulder. With his right hand on the steering wheel, he placed his left hand on top of mine.

I asked God to use the circumstances in his life to make him a better husband, a better father, and a better man. I thanked God for his sensitivity and willingness to be an example for his children, particularly his teenage son. I thanked God for placing me in this situation and for the opportunity to bear witness to the miracles he had performed in my life. I prayed all of these things in the name of Jesus.

As we came to a stop on the departure level, Mr. Davis jumped from the car, opened the door, and grabbed me in an almost painful bear hug. Passersby gawked curiously at this skinny white guy being squeezed by a large black man. He thanked me over and over for our time together. The last thing he said to me was, "I can't wait to get home and tell my wife what happened to me today!"

If you believe the circumstances I've just described are coincidences or happenstance, you are sadly mistaken. God was the supreme architect in designing each and every aspect of my relationship with Mr. Davis. God does what God does for one reason and one reason only: to bring attention and glory to himself. He often uses the circumstances in our lives to affect the people around us—even people we might think are only casual observers.

Chapter Five

MY WAYS ARE NOT YOUR WAYS

"I lie in the dust, completely discouraged; revive me by your word. I told you my plans, and you answered. Now teach me your principles."
—Psalm 119:25-26 NLT

UPON MY RETURN to Seattle, I continued to correspond with Paul. His e-mail to me in early March 2004 included the results of the February biopsy report. "Your biopsies were all negative for tumor. No cancer seen." What a relief! Once again God had answered our prayers. One more time he proved himself to be the God of miracles. For now, it seemed the course was over and God's classroom was in recess.

I settled into my work routine in an attempt at a normal life. In March I attended a men's conference sponsored by our church in Redmond, Washington. One of the speakers was Dr. Tony Evans of the Urban Alternative in Dallas, Texas. Dr. Evans' message focused on these words spoken to the nation of Israel through God's prophet Jeremiah: "'For I know the plans I have for you,' declares the Lord, 'plans to prosper you and not to harm you, plans to give you hope and a future'" (Jer. 29:11).

As I listened to Dr. Evans, I kept asking myself, *What and where are these plans God has for me? Exactly what does God expect of me after everything he has brought me through?* One statement made by Dr. Evans continued to challenge me: "Your difficulties are designed to drive you to [God]. Your pain is designed to drive you to his person, so he can reveal to you his plan. Your problems are designed to drive you to his person, so that he might unveil to you his purpose." As you'll see, I could not understand at the time the impact that statement would have upon my life.

In May 2004 a PET/CT (positron emission tomography and computerized tomography) scan was performed and subsequently reviewed with Dr. Seely in Bellevue. No sign of cancer. The results of a subsequent laryngoscopy were also unremarkable.

Throughout the rest of 2004 and into the summer of 2005, I had the opportunity to share my experiences with many, many people. Friends, relatives, business associates, and church groups listened transfixed as I shared the details of my campaign against cancer. I became a permanent part of the men's ministries teaching team at our church. My circumstances provided a wealth of material for communicating to other men the lessons God had taught me, men whom I was certain shared many of my own weaknesses and spiritual struggles.

Meanwhile, I was enjoying good health, a prosperous career, and the love of family and friends. I felt alive again. Life was good—perhaps too good.

Have you ever noticed how quickly we tend to forget where that good life comes from? Why is it so easy to be lulled into a false sense of security or a counterfeit feeling of self-sufficiency, when we are soaring on eagles' wings, running and not getting weary in our walk with God? Why do we have a natural tendency to take God for granted when we don't seem to need him? What is it about the absence of the fear factor that seems to distance us from God?

What Was I Thinking?

In late June 2005, another PET/CT scan revealed a "recurrent soft tissue mass in the right anterior pharynx, just above the hyoid [bone] … measuring 1.5 x 1.7 cm."

I forwarded copies of the report to Paul, who during the past year had moved from Baltimore to Birmingham, to take a position in the medical center at the University of Alabama. He immediately scheduled a biopsy, with the possibility of surgical resection if the mass proved malignant.

We traveled to Birmingham in mid-August. Paul performed the biopsy and was astonished that the pathology report returned negative. Had he been able to obtain a sufficient sample for testing? While we were thankful for the result, neither of us was convinced this was the end of the matter. I agreed to a follow-up PET/CT before the Christmas holiday.

A December scan revealed a mass larger than that shown on the June scan. Worse, the mass had now entwined itself around the cranial nerves responsible for swallowing, speaking, and breathing. A subsequent biopsy was consistent for "recurrent/residual squamous cell carcinoma."

The location of the tumor and its proximity to those cranial nerves took surgery off my list of treatment options. Elimination of the entire mass, with clear margins around the malignant area, would also require removing those nerves, leaving me unable to swallow, to breathe unaided, or (possibly) even speak. I was not prepared for such poor quality of life, particularly when I was in otherwise good health.

"What is it this time, God? Is this another test? Have I not learned my lesson? Is there really more for me to learn?" Rhetorical questions. Truth was, I had not forgotten or ignored the lessons. I simply had not fully implemented them into my life. What was I thinking? Failure to apply what we learn has its consequences—not the least of which requires taking the test, again.

I opened the Book, scrambling to find answers, and found what I did not want to find.

"Have you forgotten the encouraging words God spoke to you as his children? He said, 'My child, don't make light of the Lord's discipline, and don't give up when he corrects you. For the Lord disciplines those he loves, and he punishes each one he accepts as his child.'

"As you endure this divine discipline, remember that God is treating you as his own children. Who ever heard of a child who is never disciplined by its father? If God doesn't discipline you as he does all of his children, it means that you are illegitimate and are not really his children at all. Since we respected our earthly fathers who disciplined us, shouldn't we submit even more to the discipline of the Father of our spirits, and live forever?

"For our earthly fathers disciplined us for a few years, doing the best they knew how. But God's discipline is always good for us, so that we might share in his holiness. No discipline is enjoyable while it is happening—it's painful! But afterward there will be a peaceful harvest of right living for those who are trained in this way."

—Heb. 12:5–11 NLT

Discipline? Punishment? Pain? These were not words I expected or wanted to hear. They were offensive and threatening. Training, character building, even testing—these were "spiritually correct" terms I could handle. They were softer and fit more easily in my ear. Does God really use tragic situations and circumstances to punish us, his children? Does he use the pain in the lives of his creation to establish a relationship with him?

I had not abandoned my relationship with God. I was still serving him, testifying of him, and teaching about him. The problem was I had allowed my *doing* for God to become more important than my *being* with God. I was trying desperately to perform my way into God's good graces rather than returning the love that had provided his amazing grace in the first place. I had become like the church in Ephesus as described by the apostle John—I had lost my first love for God. And he wanted it back!

I recalled Miss E. J. Whately's interesting life of her father, the celebrated Archbishop of Dublin. A fact is recorded, as told by Dr. Whately, with reference to the introduction of the larch tree into

58

England. When the plants were first brought, the gardener, hearing that they came from the south of Europe and taking it for granted that they would require warmth—forgetting that they grow near the snow line—put them in a hothouse. Day by day they withered, until the gardener in disgust threw them onto a dung heap outside. There they began to revive and bud and at last grew into trees. They needed the cold.

I was about to thrown onto the dung heap of suffering in the cold climate of cancer. There my life would bud again. There I would learn another important lesson.

The words of Dr. Tony Evans echoed in my head: "Your difficulties—pains—problems are designed by God to drive you to him!"

WHY AREN'T YOU IN EUROPE?

We began 2006 with an intensified search for the latest treatment options for head and neck cancers. Paul had offered to perform a limited debulking of the tumor (leaving the cranial nerves intact) to buy me more time. He also apprised us of the possibility for using photodynamic therapy in Europe.

Europe? Why not the United States? A new drug called Foscan (*temoporphryn*), offering a higher efficacy for reaching the entire mass, was available only in Europe. More importantly, its use had produced a higher success rate.

This procedure would require travel to a foreign country, would be administered under a foreign medical program, would not be covered by insurance, and would cost somewhere in the neighborhood of fifty thousand dollars. That's some neighborhood! We decided to complete our exploration of other treatment options before making any decisions.

We found several West Coast facilities offering clinical trials for head and neck cancer treatment. Several involved the interstitial placement of chemotherapy directly into the tumor. One such trial included the direct injection of the drug bleomycin into the tumor, followed by the introduction of heat to activate the drug.

The anticipated result was ablation of the cancer. The qualifications for these trials included patients having inoperable tumors. That certainly made me a candidate.

We contacted San Diego State University to make application for one such trial and were told that a head and neck surgeon at the University of Washington was conducting the same trial at the Veteran's Hospital in Seattle. I called the doctor administering the trial; unfortunately, it was being offered only to veterans.

During our conversation the doctor said, "You are an interesting study. I've never seen a case where, after eight years, the cancer has not spread to other parts of the body." (Where had I heard that before?) He then proceeded to suggest that I allow him to surgically remove the tumor. I reminded him that the tumor was wrapped around some important cranial nerves.

"I understand your dilemma," the doctor said. "However, this may be your only chance for a cure. We have capable physical therapists at the university to assist with postoperative issues. There are times when you simply have to be willing to give up certain capacities to ensure a longer life. You really must consider letting me excise the tumor."

Had he not heard what I said? I was healthy in every other respect. At this point, I was more interested in quality of life than quantity. I was only incapacitated, in pain, inhibited, and disabled when I was undergoing some form of treatment. I graciously declined his offer.

Several weeks passed. Emotions began running hot. Even though the tumor had indolent characteristics, time was becoming more precious by the second.

We hastily investigated another procedure called radiofrequency ablation. This procedure involves placement of a special needle into the tumor using CT guidance. Radiofrequency energy is then sent through the needle, generating heat that destroys the tumor. The procedure had few, if any, side effects and little recovery time.

This sounded like the perfect solution. I immediately contacted the American Cancer Ablation Center in Gulf Shores, Alabama, and forwarded my medical records to determine candidacy for the treatment. The result? "Tumor located in an area not attainable by interstitial means." Another dead end.

In late January we began investigating recent advancements in radiation technology. While radiation is the one thing I had attempted to avoid throughout my entire experience, I wasn't certain I now had a choice. I contacted the Scottsdale Radiation Oncology Center adjacent to the Virginia G. Piper Cancer Center in Scottsdale, Arizona. We made an appointment and traveled to the Phoenix area to meet with the head of the department using Novalis® Shaped Beam Surgery—the latest in targeted radiation.

One more time I provided details of my history to the radiation oncologist. As I expected, his thinking was extremely one-sided. What I did not expect was his willingness to criticize the treatment regimens I had used in the past. "You should have had radiation in the first place," he said. "If you had, you most likely would not be here now." The doctor warned me that chemotherapy was only effective to prepare the tumor to receive radiation (I'd heard that in 1997); that surgery could only lead to bigger problems, such as recurrence or spreading of the cancer (I'd heard that in 2003); and that the application of natural methods would only serve to prolong the inevitable (I'd heard that from virtually every oncologist I'd interviewed). In his opinion, targeted radiation was the only possible cure for the cancer in my throat.

After slowly counting to ten, we informed him of the PDT process being applied with great success in Europe (confirmed by my own research). It didn't seem to faze him. "Well, if PDT with Foscan is so successful," he chided, "why aren't you in Europe?"

Seeing our emotional retreat seemed to make him realize how unfeeling his comment sounded. We thanked him for his time and turned to leave. He stopped us and said that he would not be charging us for his consultation. Small compensation for the mental anguish he had caused with a few simple words! As devastated as we were by his pronouncement, in my heart I wondered if he was right. Maybe we should go to Europe.

CANCER: A CHRONIC DISEASE?

In early February 2006, I contacted Paul and reviewed with him my research—the various clinical trials, the offer for surgery at UW, the radiofrequency ablation, and the targeted radiation. He discussed each one with me in detail.

About the injection of bleomycin, he said, "That drug can injure your heart."

He was surprised at the UW surgeon's insistence on performing a complete resection of the tumor, leaving me permanently incapacitated.

And ... "If they could reach the tumor, radiofrequency ablation would fry the cranial nerves along with the cancer."

"Radiation has always been the gold standard for treatment," he said. "Unfortunately, irradiated tissue is indistinguishable from cancer tissue, leaving successful subsequent surgery next to impossible."

As the review of my case continued, we came to a startling yet simple conclusion: the cancer afflicting my body had all the characteristics of a chronic disease. Its persistent recurrence, its non-symptomatic, slow-growing, and non-spreading nature provided evidence for such a hypothesis. As a result, our approach to treatment would have to change. Our new goals became to simply control or manage the cancer—while maintaining the best possible quality of life.

With the exception of Drs. Paul Castellanos and Daniel Seely, every physician I consulted wanted to treat the cancer in my body as a terminal illness. Each insisted the conventional chemotherapy-radiation regimens or a debilitating surgery provided the only curative treatment options—despite the fact that these methods have the highest statistical probability for threatening the patient's quality of life.

Finally, we asked Paul, "If you were in our position, and finances were not an issue, what treatment option would you choose?"

"I would go to Europe for photodynamic therapy," he answered.

We launched into a discussion of the necessary steps for obtaining the treatment. Paul confirmed his position on the leading edge of this new technology and his recent participation in a conference on the subject. He told us he had met and become acquainted with the scientists/owners of a European drug manufacturing company and offered to contact them to determine the best facility in Europe for administering PDT.

Our acceptance of his offer ignited a rapid-fire chain of events that we believed would culminate somewhere on the European continent. Our excitement yielded a confidence that God was weaving *his* plan into the fabric of our lives.

February 11, 2006. Paul sent an e-mail to Europe explaining our situation and the need for PDT with Foscan. He inquired about an appropriate facility for the procedure and even suggested the possibility that he accompany me and participate in some capacity. Paul received a response from the drug manufacturer with the names and e-mail addresses of three otolaryngologists and their respective Foscan centers in Amsterdam, London, and Orebro (Sweden).

March 1, 2006. Paul sent another e-mail to Europe with a query as to his possible role as advisor-director of my care without having formal privileges outside the U.S. He explained that he would be at a conference in Brussels during the latter half of May, making the Netherlands Cancer Institute in Amsterdam the most logistically desirable facility.

March 8, 2006. Paul e-mailed Dr. I. Bing Tan of the Netherlands Cancer Institute and described my case, asking about the use of PDT with Foscan at that facility and possible temporary privileges for U.S. surgeons in this particular PDT application.

March 10, 2006. Dr. Tan responded to Paul's request and suggested that we forward to his attention all recent head-neck imaging for review.

March 15, 2006. I investigated Dr. I. Bing Tan via the Web to acquaint myself with his credentials and the facility. I sent him an e-mail requesting the correct address for forwarding my medical files. Dr. Tan responded with the information. I was impressed with his qualifications and the facilities in Amsterdam. This looked like the right choice.

March 25, 2006. Never having been to Europe, we decided it might be wise to get some travel advice. I called my friend John, who worked for the CIA and had been on assignment all over the world—including Amsterdam. John suggested we meet for lunch. He arrived with maps, transportation options, areas of interest (as well as places to avoid), the most convenient and reasonable hotels, and his personal checklist of dos and don'ts when traveling abroad.

March 29, 2006. Paul contacted Dr. Tan to ask whether he would accept the case. He also offered a couple of dates for the procedure that would correspond with his own travel plans.

Dr. Tan responded immediately that he believed the process had potential for high success. The suggested dates would not work for him, but he offered an alternative date. Paul would only be allowed to act as an advocate. Dr. Tan also wrote that I would need a tracheotomy prior to the procedure (because PDT produces a lot of swelling around the airway).

March 30, 2006. Paul responded to Dr. Tan's e-mail with the date to correspond with his conference in Brussels and allow him to be with me for the procedure. This was exciting—God appeared to be working out every detail for us.

March 31, 2006. Dr. Tan's assistant e-mailed confirmation to Paul. Infusion of the Foscan would take place on May 11 and ablation of the tumor on May 15. We should plan to arrive in Amsterdam no later than May 10.

The requirement for a tracheotomy prior to arrival in Europe was bothersome—a messy, uncomfortable, and inconvenient procedure. Was this absolutely necessary? Despite our anxiety, a plan seemed to have come together, albeit at substantial cost. We'd have to sell a vehicle and mortgage the condo. Nevertheless, we had found a technologically equipped facility to provide the procedure and a competent physician willing to perform it. We'd been provided detailed, firsthand information about Amsterdam, and my personal physician and friend would be on hand to act as my advocate. How much better could it get—under the circumstances?

And then it happened ...

April 01, 2006. Two days before we planned to purchase airline tickets, we received an e-mail from Dr. Tan. He would not be available to perform the procedure on the scheduled dates.

This news hit like a massive blow to our emotional midsection. Now what? Paul would not be able to accompany us on the alternate dates Dr. Tan suggested. I had already changed my work schedule. Everything crumbled around us; our hopes shattered. We felt overcome with defeat. Tears flowed freely as our expectation of successful treatment was snuffed out right before our eyes.

YOU THINK YOU KNOW BEST?

Have you ever prayed for something and then mentally scripted or visualized what you believe the answer might be and the means God might use to answer that prayer? I have a tendency to subconsciously create a mental DVD of what I hope—what I want—God's answer to my prayers to look like, as well as the methods I want him to use to answer them. I am telling you from experience that my mental DVD seldom looks like the final cut of God's answer to my prayer or his plans for my situation.

Theologian J. R. Miller, as paraphrased by *Time With God—The New Testament for Busy People*, said:

> It is better we should not know our future. If we did, we should often spoil God's plan for our life. If we could see into tomorrow and know the troubles it will bring, we might be tempted to seek some way of avoiding them, while really they are God's way to new honor and blessing. God's thoughts for us are always thoughts of love, good, promotion; but sometimes the path to the hilltop lies through dark valleys or up rough paths. Yet to miss the hard bit of road is to fail gaining the lofty height. It is better therefore, to walk, not knowing, with God, than it would

be to see the way and choose for ourselves. God's way for us is always better than our own.[3]

We were learning another lesson the hard way. Fortunately we had also learned that the answers are in the Book. So, inspired by God himself, we read these verses from the prophet Isaiah: "'My thoughts are nothing like your thoughts,' says the Lord. 'And my ways are far beyond anything you could imagine. For just as the heavens are higher than the earth, so my ways are higher than your ways and my thoughts higher than your thoughts'" (Isa. 55:8–9 NLT).

We found ourselves asking forgiveness for having placed more faith in our own ability to create a plan for our lives than we had in God to work out his plan for us. This realization set in motion yet another chain of events that would prove to be more miraculous than anything we had seen so far.

April 02, 2006. Still reeling, we called Paul to discuss possible next steps. He could sense our frustration. For the first time, he had no meaningful answers. Finally, through sobs of emotional exhaustion, my wife begged, "Isn't there some way we can get the Foscan into the United States?"

Paul remembered recently receiving a copy of an e-mail between a Washington DC law firm and the Foscan manufacturer, summarizing an FDA personal-use exemption. The exemption allowed patients to bring a limited supply of an unapproved product into the U.S. for medical purposes. Paul immediately e-mailed a copy of the memo. We reviewed the material and called him. It appeared we could fly to the manufacturer's facility in Europe and bring the drug back to the U.S. under the FDA's guidelines. The only potential issue might be passing the drug through U.S. Customs.

Paul asked if we knew anyone in a government capacity who might be able to help us.

"As a matter of fact, we do. We'll call you right back," I answered.

I immediately called John, my friend and CIA operative. I quickly explained the situation, and he requested that I fax him a copy of the FDA memo. He explained he was acquainted with the head of the U.S. Customs office at Seattle-Tacoma International Airport. He promised to call back after he reviewed the memo.

Within thirty minutes John called to say, "I just spoke with my friend at Sea-Tac customs. I explained the situation, and he told me to have you call him on his cell phone if you have any problems getting the drug through the airport." Then John continued, "But I wonder why you can't simply have the manufacturer send the drug to a medical facility in the U.S.? That would certainly save you a round trip to Europe and the potential hassle of getting it through customs."

John was right. There was only one problem: could we find a facility in the U.S. that would allow the procedure to be performed using an unapproved FDA drug? We called Paul again.

"Let me contact the manufacturer and get right back to you," he replied. He immediately e-mailed his contacts in Europe and asked how fast they could export the drug and related necessary laser equipment to the U.S. The answer: as fast as we could find a medical center willing to allow the procedure to be performed using an unapproved FDA drug.

April 03, 2006. Paul began to research the possibility of obtaining permission for the procedure from the University of Alabama at Birmingham—the facility employing him as an associate professor of surgery and director of the UAB Aerodigestive Center. His research culminated in the arduous task of preparing a written request to the chairman of the UAB Health System Institutional Review Board (IRB) to provide photodynamic therapy using the unapproved drug Foscan, under the center's compassionate care provisions.

April 18, 2006. Paul faxed me a copy of his letter to the IRB chairman. The request was as complex as it was comprehensive. *Will any of this have an impact on the Board's decision?* I wondered.

April 26, 2006. I received a copy of an e-mail between Paul and the drug manufacturer confirming IRB approval—that's right, *approval*—of his request to perform PDT with Foscan at the university's medical facility. It had been only a week since the request was submitted! Paul called to personally tell us of the approval but cautioned us not to get too excited yet—there were still several ducks to be placed in a long, straight row.

Regardless, God had just confirmed that his plans are always the best—that we should never attempt to predict, forecast, or visualize what his answer to our prayers might look like. The tears flowed freely, this time tears of joy and thanksgiving for what we knew was God's perfect timing and will for our lives.

April 27, 2006. In an e-mail update to friends, relatives, and prayer partners, my wife wrote: "The doctor told David that this [approval] was really BIG! He said he hadn't wanted to dash our hopes, but that he really didn't think [UAB] would ever approve the procedure being done [in the U.S.]. We are so very grateful we don't have to go to Europe. GOD IS STILL IN CONTROL!"

Chapter Six

HOW GREAT IS
OUR GOD

"I have refined you, but not in the way silver is refined.
Rather, I have refined you in the furnace of suffering.
I will rescue you for my sake – yes, for my own sake!"
—Isaiah 48:10-11a NLT

WITH APPROVAL FROM UAB in place, we discussed with Paul the logistics for our travel to Birmingham. The procedure was placed on the operating room calendar for mid-May, and I scheduled an indefinite medical leave from my job. Paul sent me the necessary paperwork, including consent forms, requiring execution prior to admission. One phrase leaped from the page like a mongoose from a cobra: "Photodynamic therapy is an extremely painful procedure." What? There's going to be pain? OK. How bad could it be?

We were anxious to share the details of the past few weeks with our good friends Rick and Tracey Kingham, our pastor and his wife. While I described the miraculous approval by UAB to use Foscan, Rick began tapping on his PDA. "I think we can make it," he said.

"What are you talking about?"

"We're going to fly to Birmingham to be with you during treatment."

So many people emotionally committed to seeing us through our situation were praying for us, but we never imagined anyone would actually be able to physically walk with us through these circumstances. That's true friendship! We did not realize at the time how much Rick and Tracey's presence would become the support we needed, at just the time we needed it.

PET/CT and MRI scans were performed on May 3, 2006, to provide a biochemical and structural view of the tumor site, the map for proper placement of catheters into the tumor during the PDT application. The results of the scans were remarkable—the tumor *had not changed* in size or shape since December 2005 and no cancer was seen in the surrounding lymph nodes or other organs of the body. Paul reviewed the report and was amazed.

You're the Patient?

We arrived in Birmingham on Sunday afternoon, May 7. Paul met us at the airport with his entire family and transported us to the Courtyard Marriott at UAB. He informed us that the Foscan had been shipped from Europe and should arrive any day via DHL's courier service.

By Monday afternoon, however, the drug still had not been delivered. The package was being held, pending release by U.S. Customs.

On Tuesday, we visited Paul's office to determine whether we could somehow assist with getting the Foscan released. During our visit, Paul introduced us to his section chief. Looking me over from head to toe, he said to Paul, "This can't be the patient. He doesn't look sick." To me and my wife he said, "All of our patients look like they belong here. You look to be in great health. You don't look like any cancer patient I've ever seen." He continued his query about any symptoms, pains, or inhibitions caused by the tumor. He was astonished to learn that I had none. Paul and I looked at each other and smiled knowingly.

Along with Paul and his assistant, Alice, we attempted to contact DHL to determine the fastest means of having the drug released. We were passed from one agent to another until we finally reached the supervisory level. Unfortunately, the answer was the same: customs most likely would *not* release an unapproved FDA drug into the U.S.

Frustrated, I called my friend John and explained the problem. He immediately called DHL to obtain a better explanation. Apparently, the problem was one of paperwork at the U.S. Customs office in Wilmington, Ohio. John was able to get the name of the customs officer in charge.

On Wednesday we made a conference call to customs. With Paul, Alice, and me all involved in the conversation, we hoped that any questions could finally be answered. Paul explained the need for the drug. He confirmed that everything was in place for the PDT to be applied: the drug had been shipped from Europe under the FDA personal-use exemption guidelines, the medical center had approved the application of the procedure, the operating room had been scheduled for the procedure, and the patient was at the facility. We had everything we needed—except the Foscan.

The customs officer told us he had to have more data. *Of course he did.* He needed a copy of the UAB approval (a document no less than two inches thick). He needed documents describing the procedure and specifically how the drug would be administered. He needed a copy of an invoice to value the product for duty purposes. Alice and Paul scrambled to assemble the necessary data.

What was happening? Had we reached another impenetrable wall? Was God's classroom back in session? Yes. It was. We were about to learn another valuable lesson.

That evening Rick and Traccy arrived from Seattle. As they settled into their hotel room, we provided an update of the week's events. They were astonished at the seemingly ghostly attempts to thwart the process for getting the Foscan to UAB. Nevertheless, their presence provided a welcome relief from the frustrations we had faced since our arrival in Alabama.

On Thursday, Alice received a call from the customs office. This time they wanted to talk to the patient directly. That would be me. I was told I needed to provide a copy of my passport because I was the one actually importing the drug under the personal-use exemption. Of course, I did not have my passport with me. In fact, prior to our expectation that we might be going to Europe for PDT, I had no passport. Did God know I would need that passport for purposes other than travel outside the U.S.? Of course he did.

I called the property manager of our condo building in Bellevue and explained our dilemma. "I just happen to be in the building right now," she said. Following my instructions, she quickly found the passport and faxed a copy to Alice, who forwarded it to the Wilmington customs office. Now all we could do was wait. Infusion of the Foscan was scheduled to take place the next day. Would we receive the drug in time?

We spent the rest of the day with Rick and Tracey, attempting to find some distraction from our trying circumstances. During lunch, Tracey wisely advised that we now leave the situation in God's hands. After all, he really did know what he was doing. He had already proven that time and time again.

I Am The Lord!

The four of us had been invited to dinner with Paul and his family on Friday evening. That afternoon we were having a leisurely time at a nearby shopping mall when my cell phone rang. It was Alice.

"Have you talked to Paul recently?" she asked.

"No." I replied. "I haven't been able to reach him."

"Well," she continued excitedly, "if you talk to him before I do, let him know that the Foscan is on his desk."

Breathlessly I dialed Paul's cell phone and told him the good news. But his response was not what I expected. "I've had a very disturbing afternoon," he said quietly. "I don't want to talk about it over the phone. Why don't you come to the house right now so we can discuss it?"

We made our way to Paul's home in nearby Vestavia Hills. He met us at the door. His countenance was drawn and disconsolate. What could possibly have gone wrong? With tears filling his eyes, Paul began, "I'm so ashamed of myself. I don't know why it took an act of God to teach me that he is the one in control."

He explained that only a couple of hours before, he had passed his chief in the hospital hallway. He heard him say into his cell phone, "Well, here he is right now. Why don't you tell him yourself?" With that, the chief handed the phone to Paul.

On the other end of the line was the administrator for the medical center's operating rooms. Not only was she in charge of scheduling, she also had the authority to determine whether any surgical procedure could take place in the medical facility. She explained that she had just had a conversation with the university's biotechnical department concerning a special laser that none of them had seen before. Questioning the purpose for this new equipment, she was told of my scheduled PDT. "You are not authorized to perform such a procedure using an unapproved FDA drug," she informed Paul.

"I attempted to explain that I had requested and received permission from the highest authority possible—the chairman of the IRB," Paul told us. "I outlined the very meticulous steps taken to ensure that every i had been dotted and all of the ts crossed. I clarified that the drug had been released by customs, the patient was on site, and that everything was in place to apply the PDT—all in hopes of ablating a cancerous tumor." Unfortunately, the facts weren't enough to make a difference. Paul was criticized for having attempted to obtain this type of care for one of his patients. His authority, his credentials, and his character were called into question.

"I'm sorry," the administrator said, "I cannot allow you to proceed."

"Suddenly, I lost it," Paul recounted. "I told her in no uncertain terms that she was making a huge mistake—that she was not only putting the life of a patient in jeopardy, but she was also questioning my integrity." With that, the conversation had ended.

Paul said he immediately tried to reach the chairman of the IRB, who apparently was on vacation and not responding to his cell phone or pager. *What now?* Paul thought. *This is the eleventh hour. What am I going to tell the patient?*

"It was then," he added, "that I realized the real problem. I had come to believe that everything had fallen into place because of *me*. I was making it happen. I was pulling the strings. I was calling the shots. I was leading the way. I was forming the pattern. I was directing the traffic. I thought I was in control. And God was about to teach me a very important lesson."

His next step was to call his chief. Believing he had hit the speed-dial button on his phone, he expected to hear his boss's voice answer the call. "I was shocked," he said, "when I heard the voice of the hospital administrator again. I had hit the wrong button."

Not knowing what else to do, Paul slowly said, "I want to apologize for the way I spoke to you earlier."

"No," she said. "It is I who owe you an apology. You did everything required to meet the necessary protocol for getting your patient the much-needed care he deserves. The operating room is yours. You will have whatever you need to complete your mission."

Paul asked us, "Do you think God will forgive me for being so arrogant as to believe I was the one making all of this happen?"

We prayed together. Paul received the forgiveness he needed and learned a valuable lesson. I recalled the words of God to Isaiah the prophet: "I am the LORD: that is my name! I will not give my glory to anyone else" (Is. 42:8a NLT).

Paul set about to help Katherine complete dinner preparations on that warm Alabama evening, as the rest of us sat on the screened porch recalling the incidents of the day. We all agreed that Paul Castellanos would never be the same man after what God had done in his life that afternoon. Finally, I said, "If God is allowing me to go through cancer treatment with PDT here in Birmingham for no other purpose than this—it will have been worth it."

How Great Is Our God!

Early Saturday morning, Paul met us for breakfast at our hotel. He explained the process for infusion of the Foscan and what we could expect. "The only noticeable side effect of the drug itself is its photosensitivity," he explained. The drug creates sensitivity to both natural and artificial light. To prevent burning following infusion, I would have to be completely covered, head to toe, avoiding any light greater than a 60-watt bulb for three to four weeks.

After breakfast the five of us walked to the admitting desk of the UAB Medical Center and then made our way through the maze of hallways toward the hospital facility. For the first time, no one knew what to say. The highs and lows created by the events leading up to this moment had left us emotionally and spiritually exhausted.

As we rode the escalator to the hospital level, Rick began to sing the chorus of a song by Chris Tomlin: "How great is our God, sing with me how great is our God, and all will see how great, how great, is our God!" Tears filled our eyes—the anxiety melted away.

We finally arrived at the appointed room, darkened in anticipation of the side effects Paul described earlier. Just before Paul infused the drug God had miraculously brought into the country for just this purpose, Rick offered a prayer. He thanked God for having worked out his plan for our lives. He asked that the drug would do its work accordingly. He asked for a deep peace to settle upon our hearts—a peace that only God could give—the peace that is God.

The room grew eerie with silence. We watched as Paul injected the purple-colored drug into my body. The process took approximately fifteen minutes. He asked periodically whether I felt anything strange, but I felt nothing.

After the infusion was completed, I was wheeled back to our hotel room. I wore a black running suit with the hood cinched closely around my face and my hands shoved into the pockets. I wore sunglasses to keep the light out of my eyes. I looked like the Unabomber. Rick captured the event with his cell phone camera just before they said good-bye and returned to Seattle for Sunday services. We would miss them and their presence during the events to follow.

Since the drug would not be fully absorbed by the cancer cells for another three days, we spent the rest of the weekend in dark isolation. With the only light coming from the television or computer screen, we were more than bored by Tuesday. Completing even the simplest of tasks in the dark became a comedy of errors. Nevertheless, we were convinced this would be a small price to pay for successful ablation of the tumor.

WHERE ARE MY PAIN MEDS?

Around noon on Tuesday, May 16, we made our way across the sky bridge from the hotel to the hospital complex through a sea of multicolored scrubs and lab coats. After pre-op procedures, I was strapped to a gurney and wheeled into a large surgical suite.

Lying on the operating table, I was awestruck by the view. The room was stark white, and shiny, chrome-covered equipment hovered over me. After being introduced to the members of the operating team, I began deep breathing into a mask, which filled my lungs with a sleep-inducing gas. The last thing I heard was Paul's voice saying, "Don't worry. You're in God's hands now—and so am I."

Sometime on Wednesday morning I awoke in a darkened recovery room with my arms strapped to the bedside rails. I had tubes and wires protruding from, or attached to, every orifice of my body. A drug-induced state clouded my mind. No one else was in the room, and I became quite anxious about my circumstances.

The morphine given me for post-surgical pain affected my emotions as well as my ability to process the situation. My anxiety turned to panic. The panic turned to anger. Where was everyone? Where was my wife? Didn't they know I was in trouble here? Didn't anyone care about what was happening to me? I began thrashing about in my bed, trying to attract attention.

It worked. Doctors, nurses, interns, medical students, and candy stripers crowded the room. (I'm certain I noticed a custodian too.) They attempted to calm me and explain the logistics of my care. My endeavor to respond verbally resulted in a gurgling sound and the sensation of drowning. I could not seem to make anyone understand my frustration. I was given a pad and pen, and scrawled "I'm drowning!" (I wasn't, of course.) I was told to be calm and not to worry.

Be calm? Don't worry? I'm in restraints. I have a large foreign object lodged in my throat.

The breathing tube inserted during surgery had been left in as a precaution and an alternative to a tracheotomy.

OK. What about the right side of my face? It's the size of a football.

An incision, originally made in the side of my neck (used to insert the catheters), was now on the top of my cheek.

How did that happen?

Paul later explained that when the drug-saturated cancer cells were exposed to the laser light, the surrounding good tissue responded by filling up with fluid. When ablated, the cancer cells expanded to many times their original size. The combination of these reactions, of course, resulted in my face swelling—and, as promised by the surgical consent form, a lot of accompanying pain!

The subsequent removal of the breathing tube left my throat sore. When I tried to speak, the resulting guttural noises were something akin to the soundtrack of a Stephen King movie. My mind reeled. *How will I be able to communicate? It's very difficult to swallow. How am I going to eat? Why does my head ache so? My bladder feels like it's going to explode! When can I get the rest of these tubes out of my body? Why is it so dark in here? Did I actually consent to all of this? Where are my pain meds?*

My incoherent verbalizing and uncontrollable thrashing were disconcerting to my wife. She called Rick Kingham and asked him to pray with her. She wondered whether my condition would be temporary or permanent.

Paul had made eight specific passes into the tumor site to ensure treatment of the entire area. Generally, a second activation is scheduled for PDT patients to ensure complete coverage. "In your case," he said, "my goal was to take no prisoners in hope of avoiding the need for a second activation." Each of these eight ablations was like a miniature explosion that actually blew a hole up, and through, the mucosal lining of my throat. Subsequently, the body would push the dead cancer cells upward from the treated area and into my mouth for removal.

A day or so later I was moved from recovery to ICU. Adjusting to the confining darkness was difficult. My wife told me later that I performed some very strange feats while under the influence of the pain meds, including several unsuccessful attempts to get out of bed, a barrage of unnecessary and unfriendly comments fired at her and the medical staff, and the successful removal of my bladder catheter without benefit of deflation (leaving the entire medical staff in stitches). Thank God I was heavily medicated!

The next challenge was getting sufficient nourishment. Chewing and swallowing were difficult, to say the least. That meant eating foods that were either liquefied or pureed. Imagine trying to eat pureed fish! I'm not joking.

"Why can't I have ice cream and Jell-O like the other sick kids?" I cried.

"Not enough nutrients," Paul said, threatening me with a gastrointestinal feeding tube if I would not eat my pureed beef.

A couple of days later, I was moved into the hospital's general population. The darkness, postoperative pain, pureed meals, inability to sleep, and boredom were not the best prescription for a good attitude. Finally, I insisted I could fare just as well being discharged to my hotel room. Reluctantly, the doctor consented.

My meds, while providing some pain relief, gave me a buzz that kept me from getting much rest. Our only light source was still the television or computer, which made performance of various medically related activities a real challenge. The drain tube protruding from the incision in my neck required periodic clearing and emptying into a measuring cup, later used to approximate the fluid remaining at the surgical site. How long would this continue?

Since the Courtyard Marriott did not offer room service, my wife had the task of ordering take-out food from nearby eateries. Thank God nothing on the menu was pureed! I ate as much as I could in an attempt to prevent weight loss—poached eggs, oatmeal, hearty soups, puddings, and milkshakes. Not all that bad. A day or so later, Paul came by to check on me and remove the drainage tube. What a relief! I had one less thing to deal with and could shower without concern for that dangling menace in my neck.

The following day we made the trip across the sky bridge to Paul's office for an exam of my throat. The device used for this procedure was equipped with a video camera. Viewing the recording later, we were shocked by what we saw. The left side of my throat was pink and healthy. The right side could only be compared to a charred lava bed—charcoal black with sharp, jagged edges. The ablation process had quite literally burned up the malignant cells. Paul used a suction device to vacuum away the blackened pieces of dead tissue pushing up into my throat.

This attempt by my body to rid itself of the dead cancer cells would continue for several months. These eruptions produced distasteful coughing and spitting sessions, not meant for public display. Even worse was the smell of decaying tissue left on my breath.

Thank God We're Not In Europe

On May 27 we left Birmingham for Seattle. Our trip necessitated a four-hour layover in Dallas plus an airline and plane change. In anticipation of the long trek between terminals, my wife had requested wheelchairs for our arrival in Dallas and Seattle.

"No problem," said the friendly customer service representative. "We'll have one waiting for you at the gate."

We made our way off the plane in Dallas expecting to find a smiling, friendly, anxious-to-help airline representative standing behind a shiny wheelchair. You guessed it. No representative. No smile. No chair.

Now, I have a rather easygoing nature. I do anything to avoid confrontation. I always want to give people the benefit of the doubt. I'm hesitant to complain about slow service or bad work. However, when my wife believes she is not receiving what was promised her—stand back!

Many people overlook the burden placed upon the spousal caregiver when cancer strikes a family, but the effects are equally if not more devastating to the spouse. Four of the last eight years of my wife's life had been interrupted by the highs and lows of my physical struggle. She was emotionally, mentally, physically, and spiritually drained—wondering with each recurrence and treatment whether I would live or die.

In my weakened and medicated condition, I literally had to lean on her to get from the plane to the gate. The last thing she needed was a broken promise from a major airline. Of course, Terminal A at Dallas-Fort Worth was standing room only. Carolyn located the only vacant spot in the waiting area, propped me up against the wall, and headed for the counter. After several minutes she finally reached the front of the line and asked why we had no wheelchair.

Refusing to look my wife in the eye, the employee said, "In case you haven't noticed, this is the busiest airport in the country. If you will be patient, perhaps a wheelchair will become available."

This poor woman had no idea whom she was dealing with. In a voice heard and understood by everyone within earshot, my wife began to explain our plight and our need for that chair. Now lying in the fetal position, I saw her pointing at me amidst a volley of words meant to let the public know of this airline's shortcomings. "You *will* be getting a letter from me!" she shouted with a final breath. Hell hath no fury like a woman with a post-surgical, pain-medicated, physically impaired husband—and no wheelchair!

We waited for almost an hour, thinking our much-needed chair might arrive. It never did. In desperation my wife tried to hail one of those golf-cart-looking vehicles that transport needy passengers from one end of the terminal to the other.

"Do you know where we might find a wheelchair?" she asked the driver.

"Did you order one?" he replied.

"Of course we ordered one!"

Startled, he hit the accelerator and sped out of sight. Not one person, not even those witnessing our dilemma, offered any beneficial advice or assistance.

With no other option, we began making our way to the train station that would take us to Terminal E—the farthest terminal away. As bad fortune would have it, the station was at the opposite end of the terminal from our gate. No problem under normal circumstances; however, these were *not* normal circumstances.

With my wife's assistance, I took a few painful steps and then sat on the floor to catch my breath. I had taken extra medication to ease the burden. While the pill had relieved the pain, the side effects left me dazed and glassy-eyed. We bobbed and weaved our way through a sea of curious onlookers, toward the escalator leading to the station platform. *That poor woman,* they must have thought. *Doesn't he know it's unlawful to be drunk in a public place? Someone should call security!*

Our journey was interrupted by a stop at every waste receptacle, where I attempted to cough up the dead tissue pushing its way into my throat. I used all of the tissues we had brought and now could only try to camouflage my socially distasteful actions. My wife, now as much embarrassed as angry, was on the verge of collapse.

We finally arrived at Terminal E. It was three hours before our scheduled flight to Seattle. The gate area was empty. Thankfully, I was able to stretch out in the seating area for a much-needed rest.

When we were finally seated for our flight to Seattle, my wife's thoughts ran through the events of 2006 leading to this point. "What would have happened if we had pursued this process in a foreign country?" she asked." It was too horrible to imagine. "Thank God we're not in Europe!"

81

WHAT NOW?

We settled into our condo in Bellevue to continue my long recovery. My inability to consume as many calories as normal resulted in gradual weight loss and continued energy loss. The slightest physical activity left me drained and exhausted. Even the simple act of showering left me out of breath and needing a nap. My daily schedule included nothing more than moving from the bed to the couch and back again.

Boredom became our worst enemy. Did you know that with over 150 channels available on television there are very few with any redeeming value? I mean, how many times can you watch *Old Yeller*?

Recovery also included that continual and disgusting process of removing the dead tissue sloughed from my throat. After several weeks we finally wised up and obtained a portable suction device for an easier and more socially acceptable method for removing the necrotic mass.

Now, please note: the following paragraphs are rated *G* for *gross*. If you have a weak stomach, please skip to the end of this section.

A couple of weeks later, I noticed in the back of my throat a large piece of grey matter, just below the *uvula* (that little thing hanging in the back of your throat). Coughing and retching could not dislodge this strange-looking object. Frightened that this might be a sign of greater complications, I called Paul and described what I'd found.

"It's just a piece of dead tissue clinging to your throat lining," he assured me. "It will dislodge and come out sooner or later."

"What will happen if I pull it out?" I asked.

"Nothing," he answered. "Go for it."

Using a washcloth for gripping, I reached into the back of my throat and pulled out the mass. The result was a bloodied, smelly piece of gray tissue approximating the size of my thumb. I became excited by the fact that I had now opened my airway, making swallowing much easier.

I tried to share my excitement with my wife. I suggested she see what I had accomplished. She would have none of it.

"That's gross and disgusting!" she screamed from another room.

She was right. Hence, the *G* rating.

In accordance with the doctor's instructions, I placed the matter in a plastic container and sent it to the hospital pathology lab for analysis. The resulting report confirmed necrotic tissue—dead cancer cells. Disgusting though it was, the process was working.

The collateral pain resulting from the PDT extended to the base of my neck and into my right ear. As a countermeasure I was popping painkillers like they were Tic-Tacs. The only comfortable position I could find was sitting on the edge of the couch with my head in my hands.

I communicated the pain in my neck to Paul. I was surprised at his response. "Great!" he exclaimed. "That means the pharyngeal nerves are finally waking up."

All righty then!

Looking back, it seemed like an eternity before the pain finally began to subside and the daily spitting and coughing lessened. I lost thirty pounds—too much for a man already slightly built and standing six foot two. Now at 150 pounds, I was gaunt and sickly looking. Work, of course, was out of the question.

As the weeks rolled by, I slowly regained some body mass. I started eating solid food again—and plenty of it. By September I had gained back about ten pounds, and my energy level returned to around 70 percent. Nevertheless, I had a long way to go.

The days became shorter as summer faded into a cloudy, dank fall. Since I couldn't perform the required duties of my job, we made a hasty retreat to the warmth of the Arizona sun, seeking to avoid the impending dampness. There I continued to face the slow process of recovery and its accompanying boredom. I filled the hours with therapy, reading, computer use, and old re-runs of

M.A.S.H. Physical activity was still limited. Golfing (an addiction in my previous life) was out of the question—one feeble attempt left me in bed for two days.

We returned to Bellevue for the holidays and a PET scan as follow-up to the PDT. The resulting report was disheartening: "There is persistent viable tumor seen in the right neck centered at the superior aspect of the hyoid bone in keeping with a local recurrence [of squamous cell carcinoma]." Additionally, the scan revealed the possibility of cancer extending into a lymph node in the left side of my neck.

The tumor was still there? Now the cancer was in the left side of my neck? How was that possible? As if that weren't bad enough, the report also included this statement: "Persistent hyper-metabolism is seen in the region of the recto-sigmoid junction" [where the colon descends into the rectum]."

What was this all about? What was God doing this time? Why had he provided the opportunity for what should have been a "miracle cure" if it hadn't worked? Had he allowed me to go through all that pain and misery for nothing? Were we right back where we started almost a year ago? These questions, seemingly without answers, drove me into deep depression.

I discussed with Paul why the PDT did not appear to have worked.

"Apparently, the scans used to map the area for activation failed to tell the whole story," he said. "According to the radiologist, the tumor mass attacked with the PDT was hiding a secondary mass behind and below the primary tumor."

Now what?

Chapter Seven

FOR SUCH A TIME
AS THIS

"And we know that God causes everything to work together
for the good of those who love God and
are called according to his purpose for them."
—Romans 8:28 NLT

AFTER CHRISTMAS WE flew back to the Arizona sun. In January 2007 I returned alone to Seattle. Leaving Carolyn in Arizona made sense because the entire exterior of our condo building was being renovated. Windows and doors had to be removed to correct construction defects and for replacement of siding. Inside, furniture had to be moved away from all outside walls and covered to protect it from dust or damage. The only thing between me and the winter cold were large sheets of plastic.

Meanwhile, Paul had suggested a needle biopsy of the suspicious left-side lymph node shown on the November PET scan. Did he say *needle*? The instrument used for this procedure looked more like a lawn dart! As if the thought of that weren't enough, large quantifies of Novocain had to be administered (using another needle) to deaden the nerves along the path to the lymph node. Fortunately, the results of the biopsy were negative.

Good news.

At the same time, a new scan was performed to rule out speculation that perhaps previous suspicious activity in my throat was simply part of the PDT healing process. Unfortunately, the resulting report confirmed chronic cancerous activity.

Bad news.

On top of all that, the suspicious hyperactivity seen in my colorectal junction had now become a point of major concern. That would explain the periodic bleeding I was experiencing.

Worse news.

OK, I admit it. I'd never had the courage to have a colonoscopy. The mere thought of the process made me squirm like a three-year-old. I was haunted by the image of Chevy Chase trying to sing "Moon River" as he endured a rectal exam in the movie *Fletch*. I'd rather have my gums scraped! Unfortunately (or fortunately, depending upon your perspective), tests confirmed the need for the procedure. So in February I visited a colon guy for a preliminary examination.

"Yep," he said, "you really need a colonoscopy."

Just before beginning the procedure a few days later, the doctor said with a syringe in his hand, "I can give you sufficient drugs to keep you awake just enough to know what's going on or I can knock you out."

"Are you kidding?" I asked. "I don't want to hear anything, I don't want to see anything, and I certainly don't want to feel anything!"

When I awoke an hour or so later, I learned that a small benign polyp had been removed. A larger polyp was discovered just inside the anal canal and was surgically removed a few days later. It tested positive for *adenocarcinoma*—cancer in the surrounding glandular tissue.

Wonderful! I now had cancer from top to bottom, not a happy thought since both of my paternal grandparents and their siblings had all died from colon cancer. While the surgeon assured me he had successfully removed the tumor, he also warned that the cancer might have spread to my pelvic lymph system. He said that diagnostic surgery was warranted to confirm or deny the possibility.

"While exploratory, this is still major surgery," he said. "It will include removal of a large portion of your colon and the surrounding lymph nodes to determine whether the cancer has spread."

"What if you don't find any cancer in the tissue?" I asked.

"Well, then we'll know it hasn't spread," he replied.

Wait just a minute. You want me to go through major surgery, losing part of my bowel, on the possibility there might be cancer there? Was there no other test or exam for detecting the cancer?

"There is no other test or exam we can perform to determine whether the cancer has spread," he confirmed.

"Is this surgery mandatory?" I asked.

"No," he replied. "But I highly recommend it." He was adamant that the procedure be scheduled as soon as possible.

Why? Do you need a bigger yacht? Are your kids not through college yet? Are you trying to pay off your condo in Vail? Not so fast!

I decided a little more research—and prayer—were in order before consenting to a major overhaul of my plumbing.

You've Been Here Before

During the early months of 2007, I made an attempt to return to my job. A lack of strength did not allow for too many hours of work-related responsibilities. Additionally, I was not able to speak for any length of time without coughing or choking. Worse, my ability to mentally process complex transactions was lessening; in fact, this cognitive deterioration had shown up earlier in 2006—work reviewed by my business partner had proven to be inferior.

Despite everything God had done for me, the interval between cancer treatments was becoming shorter and shorter. The cumulative effects of chemotherapy, laser surgery, more chemotherapy, and PDT were leaving their mark. No one could predict when endurance levels, weight levels, concentration levels, and other functionality might return to normal. It became evident that I could no longer service my business clients in the manner they expected or deserved. After several gut-wrenching weeks, I finally realized I would have to give up the only career I'd known for some thirty years. My mind whirled as I wondered what I would do with the rest of my life.

In late February I received an e-mail from Paul with details for scheduling a surgical debulking of the tumor in my throat. Discussing the potential for success, he hinted that chemotherapy would most likely be a prudent post-surgical step, a measure intended to clean up any remaining cancer. (His suggestion did not seem unreasonable at the time.) During our correspondence I alerted Paul to the surgical procedure suggested by the colorectal surgeon.

"Oh, my," he replied. "How much more can you take? I've scheduled the tumor debulking for late April."

I called Carolyn and told her of my discussion with Paul. We agreed we would put the exploratory colon surgery on hold and travel together from Arizona to Alabama for the debulking procedure. But the day before we were to finalize our travel plans, Paul called to say that after much prayer and consideration, he had an uneasy feeling about this surgical approach. And when the surgeon has an uneasy feeling about performing surgery—sirens, whistles, bells, and buzzers should be going off in your head!

Hesitantly, Paul said, "You might want to consider chemotherapy as a pre-surgical means of shrinking the tumor away from those cranial nerves."

"Why?" I asked, pondering my prior experience with those nasty drugs.

"This surgery," he replied, "is no walk in the park. It involves some serious tissue removal—scraping the bottom of the barrel, so to speak, while trying to keep the nerves intact."

I wasn't exactly certain what he meant, but I was convinced this was part and parcel of our goal to control the chronic disease in my body. The thought of losing capacity for normal function—giving up quality of life—would be worse than the side effects of chemotherapy. Or so I thought.

I discussed this prospect with my wife. We called our friends and family. Everyone began to pray—again. One friend, who had been through a successful battle with breast cancer, told us about her experience at the Seattle Cancer Treatment and Wellness Center. "These people," she said, "treat the patient and not just the disease. They work with you to control the cancer and not simply to cure it at all costs—the cost of the patient's quality of life."

Wasn't this the same Seattle Cancer Treatment and Wellness Center I used for fractionated-dose chemotherapy in 2003? Isn't this the program I bailed from after only five treatments? What would they think if I strolled in for a second attempt? Something like, "Sorry, we don't accept quitters"?

At my wife's urging, I made an appointment to visit the center. Fortunately, the doctors and staff at the SCTWC don't turn anyone away. I was treated with the same compassion and concern I had experienced in 2003 and welcomed with open arms. Early in March we met with oncologist Dr. Nick Chen. A smile crossed his face as he reviewed the notes in my file.

"You've been here before," he said.

"Yes, I have," I replied sheepishly.

"Will you stay for the full treatment this time?" he asked softly.

Unable to look him in the eye, I responded, "That's my intent at the moment."

"I've examined your various scans and doctor's notes. We would like to give you a combination of several drugs once a week for twelve weeks. Upon completion, we'll order another scan to determine how well you are responding. OK?"

"OK," I choked.

"These drugs will also clean up any suspected colon cancer issues," he promised.

Great! Now I wouldn't have to let the colon guy cut me up.

I explained my still-weakened condition resulting from the 2006 PDT procedure. The doctor agreed to allow me a couple more months for recovery prior to chemotherapy if I promised to begin the process in early May. I said I would.

Could I keep my promise? Did I really want to voluntarily poison myself again? Would this treatment method work? What could God possibly expect me to learn from this?

In late March I completed the transfer of my clients to my business partner, said good-bye to the team I had worked with for so many years, and left for Arizona. It was a welcome relief from the drizzly weather, condo reconstruction, and reminders of the colon guy holding a scalpel in his hand. One chapter of my life was now closed. A new chapter was about to begin.

A disease called cancer had once again brought about unexpected changes into our lives. For three years we'd spent most of our time in treatment and recovery. Now, there was no job, no scheduled activities, no meaningful routine, and no anticipated future. As far as we could see, there were only months of chemotherapy and its inconveniencing side effects.

Would chemo keep the cancer in check, or had the tumor grown immune to the poison? Would this really be the beginning—or simply the end? Would I become a survivor or a statistic?

WEEK ONE

May 9, 2007. Infusion day had finally arrived. The only thing I could think about was drinking enough water to keep my body hydrated to provide a good vein for starting the IV.

I arrived at the center and cheerfully announced myself, forcing the corners of my mouth into a smile. "Good morning," I said. "My name is David Craig. I'm here to start my chemotherapy infusions."

Out of the corner of my eye, I saw a nurse coming toward me. "I remember you," she said. "You were here a couple of years ago. My name is Phu."

I remember you too, I thought, *the needle-Nazi who attacked my veins time after time with sharp, pointed objects.*

Handing me a clipboard and a pen, the receptionist said, "Please have a seat and complete these forms. Someone will call you when we're ready for you."

"Thanks," I said in a tone meant to let everyone know I was determined not to bail this time.

I found a seat and completed the required forms—questions about medical history, current symptoms, medications currently used, *blah, blah, blah*. I'd answered these questions so many times in the past ten years I could do it in my sleep.

The center's facilities were drab and dated. Walls needed freshening, carpets needed replacing, furnishings were well worn—a testimony to this organization's emphasis on people rather than property. The looks on the faces of the others in the waiting area told the sad tale—none of us really wanted to be here.

"David?" asked a male attendant.

"That's me."

"If you'll follow me, we'll get things started."

I silently followed him down the hall to a large scale standing next to the wall. I weighed in at 175 pounds, fully clothed. Next, I was seated in a small room, where my blood pressure was checked.

"Would you like a private room?" the attendant asked.

"What's my other choice?

"The group room."

Since I didn't want to be alone, I followed him to a room full of other cancer patients receiving their particular infusion on this day. The room was small—barely large enough for seven patients and the equipment needed to serve them. Just inside the door sat a small refrigerator. Next to the refrigerator was a wicker trunk full of snack foods. A water cooler stood between the refrigerator and the trunk. Hanging on the wall were posters and thatched objects meant to provide a South Seas atmosphere. Above the doorway was a sign: Tiki Room. The only thing missing was tropical-fruit drinks holding tiny umbrellas.

I situated myself in the only vacant lounge chair and waited my turn. A few minutes passed before a nurse positioned herself on a rolling stool in front of me. "Good morning," she said with a smile. "My name is Mary."

Where's Phu? I thought she would be anxious to get her hands on me again.

"You don't look like a cancer patient," she said, wrapping a tourniquet around my arm.

"Yeah, I get that a lot. What are you doing?" I asked, trying to move the conversation along.

"I'm going to place a catheter in the vein of your choice," she said.

I knew that. I was playing mind games to tolerate the process. My heart was racing as I offered her the top of my hand. The placement of the needle in the most acceptable vein signaled the start of the slow process to poison my body in hopes of controlling the cancer in my throat. *Lord, have I made the right choice?*

After a blood draw, Mary sent two vials to the lab for analysis.

I surveyed the room. The tone was quiet and somber. There were six other chairs in the room, occupied by five women and one man. I overheard a nurse call the man George. Two of the women appeared to be asleep. Two others, Karen and Linda, discussed what they would be having for lunch. The last member of the group was reading a romance novel.

Several minutes later, Dr. Chen arrived with the results of my blood work. "Are you ready for this?" he asked.

"Yes—and no."

He handed me a computer printout. There were twenty different items, each having a numerical count. Displayed beside each one was its range for normal counts. Five of them were highlighted with a yellow marker.

"These are the five numbers we will use to monitor the effects of the chemo on your body," Dr. Chen said, pointing to the printout. "If these fall below acceptable levels, we will prescribe cell-producing medicines to keep the counts up. If that fails, we may have to postpone infusion until the counts come back up within range."

He described each of the chemo drugs I would receive, their intended purpose, and their anticipated side effects. "You can expect to lose your hair around the third or fourth week," he explained. "As the drugs take effect, you will experience some digestive tract issues, acid reflux, fatigue, tingling in your hands and feet, constipation, loss of appetite, an acne-like condition on your face and neck, and nausea. These side effects will become worse as the drugs accumulate in your body. You can also expect to experience depression and chemo brain."

"Chemo brain?"

"Yes. That's what we call the difficulty to think clearly. Chemo brain," he repeated.

I'm already having problems thinking clearly. Now you're telling me the chemo is only going to make it worse? At least he wasn't trying to downplay the side effects.

He wrote a prescription for the appropriate quantity of drugs and gave it to the pharmacist on staff. Mary returned and hung a bag of "premeds"—a steroid and Benadryl as anti-nausea agents—on the IV pole next to me. After the bags emptied, she began infusion of the five drugs comprising my chemo cocktail. The completion of the process took approximately six hours.

Surprisingly, this first infusion didn't seem too bad, as long as I didn't consider the sleep depravity resulting from the steroids, the severe burning in my upper digestive tract caused by the 5-FU, the weird metallic taste in my mouth produced by the combination of drugs, or the constant buzzing in my head. Otherwise, the days until the second infusion were uneventful.

WEEK TWO

The night before the second scheduled infusion, my wife and I watched the movie *One Night with the King*, the story of Esther, a Jewess, chosen to be the unlikely wife of a Persian king. Through a series of God-ordained circumstances, Esther was placed in the perilous role of pleading with the king for the lives of her people. While pondering this potentially deadly encounter, she was counseled by her uncle, who told her that God had quite likely elevated her to the role of queen "for just such a time as this." Because of her courage and faith in God, Esther's request was granted and her people were saved from annihilation.

On May 16, with the details of Esther's story fresh in my mind, I drove myself to the center to get my drugs. For the record, the Tiki Room, despite attempts to make it appear otherwise, was not a happy place. Sure, we smiled, offered pleasantries, and occasionally laughed out loud. But no one was fooled. Yes, it was a place of hope, but mostly of hopelessness. It was a place full of people, but mostly of emptiness. If you looked closely enough, the painful threat of death by cancer could be seen in the eyes of every victim. Without God's intervention, this horrifying disease would make a statistic of many.

After the usual preliminaries, the first drug began dripping its way into my bloodstream. At this point Linda asked, "So, what are you in for?"

Minutes later, I was startled by the silence. No one was speaking—except me. I'd just spent that time telling a group of strangers many details of the last ten years of my life. My partners in chemo (and the nurses serving them) now knew my medical and personal history. Some of them were awestruck. Some were skeptical. Some of them cried. Some were silent. No one could believe I was still alive to tell the story.

Looking into these desperate faces, I now understood why God prompted Paul (without his knowing it) to suggest I consider chemotherapy as a pre-surgical protocol. I was not here by accident. It was no coincidence that Linda asked her question. These hurting, searching people needed to hear a testimony of God's healing power. They needed to know of another battle plan for defeating the horrible disease attacking their bodies.

In the midst of my self-pitying, whiny, what-about-me attitude, God spoke into my heart. The answer to the "why" question suddenly became obvious. God had enrolled me in the fractionated-chemo program at SCTWC "for such a time as this"!

In the days that followed, the doctors' predictions concerning the chemo side effects began to come true. The most noticeable and most bothersome was the burning in my esophagus. There seemed to be no relief from that hot, painful sensation. The tissue in the lining of my digestive tract was being destroyed faster than my body was able to replenish it, making eating a challenging and undesirable situation. Yet I needed nourishment to aid my body's ability to stave off the poisonous effects of the drugs.

The steroids given to combat the side effects created other problems. They kept me awake, left me agitated, and made me aggravated. I was not pleasant to be around. My primary caregiver, my wife, was equally unhappy with the situation as my disposition deteriorated—and it was only the second week.

I prayed, "Dear Lord, if you have truly placed me in these circumstances for a purpose, I'm going to need your help to get through them. Please reveal yourself in a mighty way and give me the mental, emotional, physical, and spiritual strength necessary to accomplish that purpose."

WEEK THREE

As part of its patient-first philosophy, the SCTWC staff included naturopathic physicians and holistic treatment (such as acupuncture) providers. Its goal to treat the patient, not just the disease was evident time and time again.

My third infusion day on May 23 was no exception. One of the clinic's naturopathic doctors visited me. She recommended a specific diet and dietary supplements to support my body's immune system and counter the anticipated side effects of the chemo. I assured her that none of these recommendations was unfamiliar; I had maintained a strict diet and supplement routine for many years. This lifestyle had proven to be a key component for managing the cancer in my body and keeping the chemo side effects to a minimum.

Mary arrived to start my IV. For reasons still a mystery this was the most difficult step of the infusion process for me. The doctor called it *belonephobia*, the fear of pins and needles. My wife called it baloney. No matter the reason, I still found it *painful*! Particularly when the veins were not cooperating and it took more than one attempt to get the needle in, the catheter threaded, and the saline flowing.

95

With the premeds finally dripping, I settled down to eat my lunch—a deli turkey sandwich on wheat bread. Before I could finish, my head started falling onto my chest as the Benadryl kicked in. *Oops! Was I snoring?* Not for long. The steroids were next, and the resulting buzz had me talking faster than a campaigning politician. The nursing staff seemed to find this change in my demeanor amusing. *Ha-ha-ha!* Finally, the first chemo drug was introduced.

Many patients were accompanied by a spouse, adult children, or a friend. Since I lived only eight miles away, I traveled alone to and from my appointments. Ellen came from over one hundred miles away for her weekly infusion. Her best friend, Barb, drove her both ways. Now that's friendship.

George had a visitor today, a former patient named Rob. Rob said he was given the same drug regimen prescribed for me and that he had to quit after only seven infusions. Apparently he could not tolerate the side effects of the Erbitux. "Erbitux makes you break out with an acne-like condition," he told us. "My face was completely covered with small pus-filled sores. They burst and bled, leaving my face a mass of exposed nerve endings. The pain was so severe, I simply couldn't take it any longer."

Listening with wide-eyed curiosity, I was disheartened when Rob assured me I could expect the same thing to happen in the coming weeks. *Thanks Rob.* Later that day, Dr. Chen confirmed what Rob had said. In fact, the doctor was surprised I'd not yet had some reaction.

By the end of the week, the side effects of my chemo cocktail began to expose themselves to an even greater degree. I had no energy. I didn't want to get out of bed. The steroids only compounded my problems, keeping me on a high for up to thirty-six hours. When the stimulant finally wore off, severe acid reflux interrupted my sleep. Along with the destruction of tissues in my digestive tract, I developed a chemo-induced sliding hiatal hernia—a condition in which a portion of my stomach pushed its way up and through my diaphragm and down again.

Prior to each infusion, Dr. Chen discussed the side effects I'd experienced during the prior week and made recommendations for specific supplements or prescription medicines to help counteract them. His biggest concern was my blood cell counts, consistently dropping each week.

Eating was becoming more difficult. My body's attempt to digest food was painful. Once digested, I experienced a short, pain-free window, but only until the process of elimination began. Since my body was unable to adequately digest the food, severe constipation resulted. Can you feel my pain?

I had a constant burning in my upper abdomen. I tried lying very still so as not to arouse the chemicals in my body. A heating pad provided some degree of relief. The most comfort came from gently rubbing my stomach. It was quite a sight—a grown man rubbing his tummy and groaning softly. *Make the pain go away!*

WEEK FOUR

Despite the welcome sunshine of this late spring day in May, my attitude was not the best. In fact, it was downright nasty. I didn't want to do this anymore. All I could think about was how much worse the pain would get.

My drive to the infusion center followed a route across majestic Lake Washington and through a tree-lined arboretum—a beautiful drive under normal circumstances. In the backwater of the lake, a couple in a canoe paddled lazily through the lily pads. What were they smiling about? Didn't they know I had cancer? Didn't they know the emotional and physical pain I was suffering? How could they be so happy?

Free parking was available to patients of the center—if you could find an empty spot. Having to drive around the lot three times before one finally came available worsened my already bad disposition.

I accepted the clipboard and pen from the receptionist without a word and plopped myself in a chair as far away as possible from the other patients. I checked the boxes concerning the side effects and pain experienced during the past week. Responding to the question about my mental and emotional state, I printed in large bold letters, WHAT DO YOU THINK?

My name was called, and I followed the attendant down the hall. He could tell by the look on my face how I was doing and wisely knew better than to ask. He checked my blood pressure, and a frightened look crossed his face. "Your blood pressure is alarmingly high," he said. "Are you having any problems?"

"Do you mean other than the fact that this is the last place on earth I want to be right now?" I snapped.

He nodded. I was not the first patient to have abused this innocent bystander whose only goal was to help me. *I owe him an apology—maybe later. Right now I really don't care. I just want to have this over!*

I made my way to the Tiki Room. *I'd better not have to wait for a chair—and I want the one in the corner!* I found my place and set up my computer to journal my experience. A nurse, Susan, rolled herself in position next to me.

"Good morning," she said with a smile. "Are you ready for me to start your IV?" *What do you mean? Where's Mary? I just got her trained, and now I get a stranger?* "Mary has changed her schedule. She won't be here on Wednesday mornings," Susan said cheerfully as she attempted to insert a needle into the top of my hand.

That just made my day. Needing three attempts (that's right, *three*) Susan finally found an accepting vein and inserted the catheter. After drawing what seemed like a couple of gallons of blood, Vampira—I mean, Susan—sent it to the lab. She started the drip and left me to stew in my own premeds. Several minutes went by and Dr. Chen brought me a copy of the lab report. He had a look of concern on his face.

"Your white counts are dropping way too fast," he said. "I'm going to prescribe a cell-producing medicine you'll have to take for a couple of weeks. The drug is called Neupogen. We'll dispense it from here. You will get three vials for self-injection over a three-day period."

"Did you say self-injection?"

"Yes. Is that a problem?"

"Of course not," I said, lying through my teeth. Didn't these people know by now how much I feared and hated needles? Now I had to intentionally jab one into my abdomen on a daily basis? *Lord, take me! Take me now!*

I know what you're thinking—*What a big baby! It's just a little, tiny stick with a little, tiny piece of sharp, pointed metal. Get over it!* I know linebackers who are afraid of itsy, bitsy spiders—so leave me alone about the needles, OK?

The side effects continued to plague my body for the five days following infusion. By the sixth day I actually started to feel a little better—just in time to go back for more poison.

Week Five

While the Neupogen had stabilized my white cell counts, they were still dangerously low. Dr. Chen gave me another prescription for three more injections. "If this doesn't get your counts up to normal," he said, "we will have to give you a break from the chemo."

Really? A break? Maybe I should refuse the medication and take the week off? Of course that would only prolong the agony.... I'll take the medicine.

Waiting for my pre-meds, I noticed an unfamiliar man entering the room. He was tall, gaunt, hunched over, and moving slowly. Holding onto the arm of a young woman, he found an empty seat two chairs away from me. I watch curiously as the woman held his hand and seated herself next to him. She set a lunch sack on his table tray. The name Larry was printed neatly on the sack. I couldn't know at the time how Larry would impact my life.

While the composition of the Wednesday infusion group changed from week to week, the one face I knew I would see belonged to George. We'd become close companions during the six hours we spent together each week. We shared our cancer experiences, our research, our approach, our attitudes, and even our lunch. We took turns bringing sugar-filled doughnuts and cookies on infusion day. (Consumption of these otherwise prohibited foods was encouraged by the oncologist as a means of stimulating the cancer cells subsequently exposed to chemotherapy.)

George was also afflicted with cancer in his throat. His tumor, now the size of a golf ball, was protruding from the side of his neck. He was in his second twelve-week cycle of fractionated dose chemotherapy. He had been investigating targeted radiation as a means of eradicating the tumor. One local clinic was not willing to treat him unless he consented to full-field radiation. George was appropriately concerned about the side effects of wide-field gamma ray bombardment.

I told him about the many times I had rejected radiation as a treatment option. I too had read and heard gruesome stories of resulting incapacitation: the severe pain of cumulative treatments, loss of taste and salivary function, subsequent dental issues, loss of jawbone and support structures, and scar tissue that can preclude subsequent surgery.

"You are very strong," he said. "I don't know too many people with the courage to take control of their medical treatment the way you have—especially cancer treatment. Most people do what the doctor says simply because he's the doctor and ... well ... the doctor knows best."

"I'm very fortunate," I replied. "The doctor who first diagnosed my cancer in 1997 witnessed the disappearance of the tumor after only two cycles of chemo. While he didn't agree with my refusal of further chemo and radiation, he continued to be involved in my case when he saw the level of our faith and the obvious miracle God performed. He has since acknowledged many times that I made all the right decisions for controlling the cancer—including my refusal to expose myself to radiation."

Holding a heating pad next to the tumor on his neck, George listened intently. I promised to pray for him. While he was grateful for my concern, he seemed skeptical that something as simple as prayer could help him. Our conversation was interrupted by the nurse assigned to begin his infusion. I continued to pray for George and his fight to gain freedom from the disease holding him in its grip.

For most of the afternoon, we sat in quiet contemplation. George continued his research on the Web as I journaled my thoughts and observations of the day. Every second was marked by a steady *drip, drip, drip, drip* as each drug in succession found its way into our bloodstreams, one poisonous drop at a time.

On the drive home my heart pounded. I realized I now equaled the number of infusions I had reached in 2003. I was becoming quite ill from the plethora of poisons. *This is why I quit four years ago*, I remembered.

Would the dietary supplements and medications help my body control the effects of the drugs? Would God help me get through this horrible experience—since (I was convinced) he had led me here in the first place? Would I return for a sixth infusion? Could I make it through the next seven weeks? If I did, would it make any difference?

Chapter Eight

YOU TRUST ME,
I RESCUE YOU,
YOU GLORIFY ME

*"Fire tests the purity of silver and gold,
but the LORD tests the heart."*
—Proverbs 17:3 NLT

WATER SPATTERED ONTO my back and steam quickly fogged the glass panels of the shower. The water's warmth brought temporary soothing to my sore, aching muscles. Unfortunately, a shower was not a daily event. It took all of my energy just to soap, shampoo, rinse, and dry. As a result, I didn't always make the effort.

On this particular occasion the shampoo cycle produced a handful of hair. "I'm losing my hair!" I yelled.

"Well, the doctor said it would happen," Carolyn hollered back.

"But I don't want to lose my hair," I whined.

"It will grow back," she scolded.

I'd always been able to mock my younger brothers for having thinning locks and receding hairlines. My mane was always thicker and more luxurious.

"I don't care," I said, "and how do you know it will grow back? You're no doctor!"

I was wasting my breath. I knew she was right. I was feeling sorry for myself and I didn't care who knew—another one of the not-so-often-discussed side effects of chemotherapy, self-pity. Let me assure you, it does exist. For all the stories of brave cancer victims toughing it out through the horrors of chemo, there are just as many of us behind the scenes who don't—or won't—grin and bear it.

Problems for our human species always seem to occur in multiples, and each generally overlaps the other. As if illness produced by chemotherapy, my poor disposition, and losing my hair weren't enough, my wife now needed surgery of her own. A partial hysterectomy performed weeks earlier in Arizona had not accomplished all she'd hoped. As a result, she was admitted to the hospital for completion of the process. Suddenly our roles were reversed—the patient was now the caregiver and the caregiver was now the patient. In my weakened and sickly condition, I sucked it up and got her to and from her appointments.

In an e-mail update to family and friends, Carolyn described our situation:

June 10, 2007

> David is doing OK, so he picked me up [from the hospital] yesterday. Now we both walk slowly around the house. I can still out-shuffle him though. He sits rubbing his stomach because of the chemo pain and I walk around holding mine. Can't you just visualize that?

The next day I called our friend Rick Kingham—a man of many trades, including that of barber. "My hair is coming out in handfuls," I declared. "Can you come over and cut it off so I won't have to find it on my pillow?"

He was all too eager to accept my offer. He not only brought his shearing equipment but four different hats and caps. What a guy! I might be bald but I wouldn't be cold. I was certain I had him convinced to buzz cut his own head as a show of solidarity. Alas, it was not to be. As my locks hit the floor with each pass of the razor, I was certain I heard the sound of "Taps" somewhere in the distance.

WEEK SIX

My infusion time on June 13 was earlier than usual—8:45 A.M. George arrived shortly after me. We exchanged greetings, completed the requisite paperwork, and discussed the previous week's side effects and impact to our daily lives. In turn, we made our way to the Tiki Room.

Jessica was my nurse on this day. I'd finally learned that I was assigned the nurse who happened to grab my folder from the top of the pile. We exchanged pleasantries, and she offered me a heating pad to entice the veins in my hand. *Lord, please allow my veins to be receptive today—and help Jessica to get it right the first time!*

It worked! The needle stick was barely noticeable, and the catheter threaded nicely. Jessica drew some blood and took it to the lab.

"You came back!" Dr. Chen exclaimed, walking into the room.

Sitting down with my lab reports in one hand, he thrust the other toward me, saying, "Congratulations! We weren't certain you would actually make it this far."

Oh? Who won the pool? What kind of odds was I getting? "I'm as surprised as you are," I replied, shaking his hand. Removing my hat, I said, "I figure as long as I have to look like this, I might as well finish the job."

"No hair," he laughed, rubbing my head.

"Welcome to the club," said Karen. "You are now an official member of the bald brigade."

"Tell me about your side effects," the doctor said.

I listed them: the esophageal burning, the steroid highs, the facial flushing, the fatigue, the chills, the tingling in my feet and hands, the constipation, the aching in my bones, and the mental anguish. I complained about the least little problem. After all, he asked.

"I'm not surprised," he said. "Your red blood cell count has dropped to the bottom of its normal range. We will be watching it very closely. If it gets much lower, we may want to give you some

Procrit." I wanted to avoid that if at all possible. Procrit is a red blood cell producing agent given by injection in the underside of the upper arm. We all knew my feelings about another injection.

I finished my premeds, and Jessica attached the first bag of chemo to my IV. I heard a commotion and noticed Larry making his way into the room. This time he was accompanied by an older woman, presumably his wife.

"Good morning, Larry," I said with a smile as he was helped into his chair.

"Good morning," he replied, wondering how I knew his name.

"It's Larry, isn't it?"

"Yes," said his wife, with the same puzzled look on her face. "What's your name?" she asked.

I identified myself and quickly told them about seeing Larry's name neatly printed on his lunch sack the week before. A look of relief crossed their faces. Larry's wife explained that their daughter had packed lunch for both him and his granddaughter, dutifully printing their names on the sacks.

As we discussed our reasons for being in the group room, she told me Larry had the same type of cancer I did and was on the same chemo regimen. She said that Larry was not tolerating the drugs very well. He did not eat regularly because the resulting vomiting and diarrhea were more than he could bear. "He's lost another four pounds this week," she said. "He's lost a total of thirty pounds in three weeks. I don't know if he can continue the chemotherapy."

I was suddenly ashamed of myself. Sure, I had my problems, but they didn't include an inability to eat, and I wasn't losing weight. *Lord, forgive me for my selfish, self-absorbed, pitiful attitude.*

Larry's nurse began administering his first set of drugs. Moments later, Larry's head dropped to his chest. His eyes were closed and his body went limp.

"Larry, are you OK?" the nurse asked.

No response. The staff sprang into action. Dr. Chen checked Larry's vital signs: his blood pressure was dropping and his pulse was weak. A team of nurses surrounded him and began giving him oxygen.

"Larry, can you hear me?" the doctor shouted.

No response.

I was overcome with emotion as I watched this scene. Every eye was fixed on Larry, many filled with tears and all with a look of fearful anticipation. Were we witnessing the passing of a fellow cancer victim? But for the grace of God, that could be me! *Lord, touch Larry's life right now. Don't let him die. Use these circumstances to show him his need for you.*

A few moments later Larry regained consciousness.

"Are you dizzy?" the doctor asked. Larry nodded.

A collective sigh of relief could be heard and felt throughout the room. Larry was wheeled to a private area, and paramedics arrived to transport him to the hospital.

I never saw Larry again.

WEEK SEVEN

If it were possible, the side effects of the chemo were getting worse. I could see and feel the change in my body chemistry from the destruction of red blood cells. I was willing to try anything to repair the damage and find relief from the misery. Dr. Chen had repeatedly suggested I try the ancient art of acupuncture. You know, the art of sticking dozens of little *needles* into your body. For several months my granddaughter had visited an acupuncturist for treatment of various neurological issues, with positive results.

"If your granddaughter can stand having teeny tiny needles inserted into her skin, certainly you can too," my wife chided.

I wasn't certain which was worse: having my manhood challenged or suffering the side effects of chemotherapy. I didn't understand how the placement of needles in my scalp, face, chest, wrists, knees, and ankles could possibly help. But I was desperate.

Nicole was professional, sensitive, and caring individual. She was correct when she told me acupuncture was really a painless process. Even greater than its relief of many side effects of the chemo, acupuncture helped me cope with my fear of the needle. Visiting Nicole for acupuncture treatment became a weekly routine following each infusion. I actually looked forward to the event almost as much as my visit to the chiropractor.

On June 20, after the usual preliminaries, Dr. Chen visited me to discuss my blood counts. "I'm afraid your red blood cell count has dropped out of range," he said. "We're going to have to give you the Procrit to get them back up."

Maybe my fear of needles wasn't completely gone. "Isn't there any alternative?" I asked. "What about dietary changes or supplements? Can't I do something myself to get the counts back up?"

Dr. Chen described the various leafy vegetables and other foods I could eat to encourage red blood cell growth. I also learned these cells are reproduced in bone marrow, and that walking and exercise encourage such reproduction.

"Let's make a deal," I suggested. "Give me a week to get the counts up, and then we'll talk about the Procrit." Hesitantly, the doctor agreed.

He then asked me the usual questions about side effects. I described the problem of trying to sleep during the day and a half following infusion. "Exactly how many milligrams of steroid am I getting?" I asked.

"Twenty," he replied. "If you like, we could cut it in half and see how that works."

"I'll do anything to get a better night's sleep," I said.

The doctor left the room, and I settled myself into position to receive the week's infusion. It was taking longer than usual to get started; two nurses had called in sick, so Jessica and Lisa had to service twice as many patients. Finally, the first drug started dripping into my body. After an hour or two, they finally attached another bag of chemo, and I was left to my writing in an attempt to pass the time.

Another hour passed. I looked at the bag hanging on the pole to my right. Strange—the fluid level hadn't dropped at all. Something wasn't right. The bag should be half empty by now.

"Excuse me," I said to Lisa as she passed by, "I think there is something wrong with my IV line. My chemo bag is not dripping properly."

Disgruntled, Lisa stopped to look and fumbled with the line attached to the bottom of the bag. Suddenly, the bag burst open and its contents spewed onto my head, running down my face and arms. My skin began to burn.

Lisa screamed sharply, "Chemo spill! Chemo spill!" A look of terror was in her eyes.

Immediately the room filled with nurses, attendants, and other team members. All patients were evacuated to outer areas of the facility. Lisa soaked a towel with water from a nearby sink and began wiping me down. She ordered me to remove my clothing. *Remove my clothing?*

My hair was wet with the foul-smelling drug. The IV line was removed from the catheter in my arm, and I was ushered to the corner sink for a further dousing. "We have to neutralize the chemo," Lisa said, sobbing. "Does your skin burn?"

Just then two nurses burst into the room clad in protective canvas suits, their heads covered with clear plastic shields to protect them from the poison. Using equipment designed to clean up hazardous waste, they worked to contain the toxic mess.

"Did you get any chemo in your eyes?" they asked.

Thankfully, I was wearing glasses while using my computer. I could see through their face shields a look of relief as I assured them my eyesight was not affected. God was watching over me, no question about that.

Standing in a corner, my bald, pasty, skinny body clad only in boxers and a sheepish grin, I realized I was the calmest person in the room. Lisa was an emotional mess.

"I'm so, so sorry," she blubbered. "I don't know what happened. All of a sudden there was chemo everywhere."

"It's OK," I said. "I don't blame you. It was an unfortunate accident."

Finally, everyone was satisfied that the clean-up process was a success, and I was given a pair of blue scrubs to wear. The other patients returned to the room, and everyone wanted details of the event. For a moment, I felt like a rock star. The only thing missing was a guitar and the crowd mouthing my every word.

Dr. Chen interrupted my fifteen minutes of fame when he stopped by to examine me. He wanted to be certain I had suffered no permanent damage from the spill and, I suspect, to forestall any potential litigation regarding the same. He told me to go home and return the next day to complete my infusion.

Great! I have big plans tomorrow. I don't remember exactly what they are—probably rubbing my stomach and trying to cope with the buzz in my head—but I'm certain they don't include coming back here for more drugs!

WEEK EIGHT

The next day I returned to the center to complete my infusion. Since this was not my usual day, the occupants of the Tiki Room were unfamiliar to me. I found an empty lounge chair and introduced myself to my neighbors. A few moments later I heard a familiar voice. Mary!

"It's so nice to see you again," she declared. "I hear you were quite a hit around here yesterday."

Everyone heard her comment. Immediately, I was the center of attention.

"How did it happen?"

"Did you get burned?"

"Where did it touch you?"

"Were you frightened?"

Since I had nothing but time, I proceeded to describe in great detail the events of "the day the chemo bag burst." Surprisingly, I had no physical evidence of the spill. There wasn't even redness where the chemo had touched my skin. I alerted my audience to the fact that God's protecting hand was upon me during an otherwise disastrous event.

I completed my infusion and returned home to concentrate on ways to get my red blood cell counts up. Despite my fatigue and the aching in my bones, I determined to walk every day. The next morning I threw on my sweats and cap and ambled several blocks up the street and back again.

Besides the physical benefits, this time alone proved spiritually profitable as well. In the quiet of the morning, I was able to hear God speak to me more clearly than ever before—or maybe I was simply listening more closely. I was able to see God in ways I'd never seen him before—or maybe I was simply looking more closely. Our walks together quickly became the most powerful time of my day. These encounters helped me understand God's real purpose for sparing my life—he was not finished with me yet!

My wife and I prepared a shopping list and traveled to Whole Foods to find those leafy greens intended to build red blood cells. Kale, arugula, and spinach became the main ingredients in our morning omelets. Not the best tasting, but I was desperate.

I visited Nicole for my weekly acupuncture treatment and told her about my blood count drop. She suggested adding quinoa (a high-protein grain) and blackstrap molasses to my diet. Additionally, the nutritionist at SCTWC recommended a helpful vitamin supplement.

All of these lifestyle changes were beneficial. However, the most important supplement to my daily regimen was prayer. I constantly reminded God of who he was (as if he needed me to remind him) and of his power to use the methods I'd employed to increase my red blood cell counts. Think of the testimony I would have if my red blood cell counts went up in just one week!

Heading toward the shower after my morning walk, I caught a glimpse of myself in the bathroom mirror. What was that all over my face?

"Carolyn!" I shrieked. "Come here and look at this." My face was covered in tiny, raised bumps.

"Uh, oh. It looks like the doctor was right. You're finally having a reaction to the Erbitux."

I recalled my conversation with George's friend Rob about his reaction to the drug: "The pain was so severe I had to quit after seven treatments." Rob's words reverberated back and forth in my head like echoes off a canyon wall.

I located the literature the doctor had given us concerning this new chemo drug and read, "The most common side effect that can be caused by Erbitux is an acne-like rash. The rash usually occurs on the face, upper chest, and back, and may cause itching."

I hadn't noticed any rash on my chest. "Do I have anything on my back?"

"Not yet."

Maybe this was the worst it would get. Maybe I wouldn't have the same problems Rob had. Maybe I'd escape the plague of the poison. I only had a few more weeks to go. Could I make it to the end or would I bail, after all? This pain and misery had better have a purpose.

My journal for July 11 reads, "Dear Lord ... I am absolutely certain you have allowed the cancer in my body to remain a chronic ailment ... for a purpose. The apostle Peter was right when he wrote, 'When your body suffers, sin loses its power; and you won't be spending the rest of your life chasing after evil desires, but will be anxious to do the will of God'" (1 Peter 4:1-2)

No question about that. The furthest thing from my mind right then was doing anything that might disappoint the God who had spared my life.

Time was moving slower with each passing day; July 5, my eighth infusion—only four more to go. My energy level seemed to have stabilized. I'd been faithful to my daily walk and talk with God. I was confident my red blood cell counts hadn't decreased any further.

The routine was the same—check-in, paperwork, weight and blood pressure. I meandered into the Tiki Room and found a seat next to George. He updated me on his search for radiation treatment. He was not encouraged by the results. I was concerned for George and not really able to do anything tangible for him. I could only offer words of encouragement and prayer for him. Often, that's more than enough. Most people in pain simply need an attentive ear.

After a blood draw, Dr. Chen visited me with the results of my cell counts.

"What's up, Doc?" I asked jokingly.

"What have you been doing?"

"What do you mean?"

"Your red blood cell counts have gone up!"

"How is that possible?" George asked.

My heart was thundering so hard I was certain it could be heard for several blocks in every direction. I had hoped the counts wouldn't decrease any further. I never imagined they would actually go up. God had performed another miracle!

"What have you been doing?" the doctor asked again.

"Talking to God," I declared.

"That's all?" he asked with a voice of astonishment.

"No. I've been eating my leafy greens, walking, and following the instructions of my medical team. But, mostly, I've been talking to God."

"Well, whatever you're doing, it's working. I fully expected to find your red cell count down from what it was last week. It looks like we won't have to give you Procrit."

"Hallelujah!" I exclaimed.

"Congratulations," George said.

"Did the reduction in the steroid quantity help you sleep better?" the doctor asked.

"No. Any chance you could lower the dosage even more?

"Are you having any nausea the day of your infusion?"

"No."

"OK, then we will reduce the dose by four more milligrams."

The doctor noticed the rash on my face and commented that it had taken longer than usual for this side effect to manifest itself. He told me I was fortunate that the condition was not any worse.

George was listening to our conversation with heightened interest. After the doctor left and we were hooked up to get our drugs, George commented again on the miraculous increase in my red blood counts. "I've never heard of anything like that before," he said. "You really believe in prayer, don't you?"

"Yes, I do, George. That's the only reason my counts went up. There is no other explanation. Medically, all of my dietary and lifestyle changes could only have stabilized the counts. It is God who answers my prayers and works out the details of my life."

"I believe he does."

"He can do the same thing for you, George."

George became quiet and hid himself behind his laptop. Perhaps I would have another opportunity to engage George about God's desire to touch his heart. Suddenly I was reminded again that God had placed me in this situation "for such a time as this."

WEEK NINE

I walked slower but longer each day, pushing myself because I was determined to keep my blood counts up without chemical assistance. My conversations with God revolved around continuing chemotherapy. I'd completed eight infusions. Did I really need four more? I felt sick all the time, I'd lost a couple of toenails, my hair was gone, and the rash on my face was getting worse. When I walked into a public place, small children ran screaming to their mothers. How could this be a good thing? What lesson was God trying to teach me now? Hadn't I learned everything he had for me? I needed a rest from all of this.

Trying to rationalize away the necessity for more chemo, I found myself puzzled by the basis for the number of infusions used in this treatment regimen. Why not six, or eight, or nine? What was so magical about twelve? Why wouldn't we want to obtain a scan each month or two to determine the progress of the chemo? If the tumor was gone, why would I continue to put myself through all this?

I had now experienced virtually every side effect promised by the oncologist. They were piled high, one upon the other, and worsening with each passing day. "I don't think I can do this anymore," I cried to my wife.

"Only four more treatments," she said quietly. "The doctor said you had to have all twelve infusions."

"But why? Why does the formula require twelve? I don't know if I can take it any more."

"I know," she said sympathetically. "God will help you through it. You just have to trust him"

Trust him? Of course I trusted him—it would just be nice to know that I was going through this for the right reasons. What if, after all the pain and discomfort, the tumor was still there? What then?

Reading God's Word is an essential and necessary part of an intimate relationship with him. The Bible not only helps us understand who God is but what God does. It's impossible to hear God, or to listen to him, without knowing what he is saying. The Bible is God speaking—it is his words to us. It is the book that must be opened to find answers to the tests in life. I was determined to find the answers to my questions and my circumstances. I read these words from Psalm 50:15: "Trust me in your times of trouble, and I will rescue you, and you will give me glory" (NLT).

These three word phrases leaped off the page:

You trust me!

I rescue you!

You glorify me!

The words didn't immediately answer my questions, but would certainly affect my perspective. Two of those three commands required action on my part. God was saying to me, "You are to trust me and only me, I'm the one, the only one, who will rescue you. All of the credit for the rescue must be given to me. It's all about *me*!"

July 11. I wasn't certain I would have any more infusions. I'd discuss it with the doctor, but he was going to have to convince me I absolutely needed more chemo.

"The nurse tells me you've refused an IV today," Dr. Chen said.

"That's right. I need to know why it's necessary to have more chemo. How do we know that the treatment hasn't already shrunk the tumor? Why don't we have a PET scan performed to confirm the progress of the treatment?"

"Because," he said, "this is the way it's always been done."

Gong! Wrong answer! Want to try for double jeopardy, where the answers really get tough? "What do you mean by that?" I asked.

"Well, we've never prescribed less than twelve infusions."

"Has anyone ever asked this question before?"

"No."

"I'm sorry, Doctor. I'm struggling to find the motivation to finish this program. Are you telling me that without all twelve infusions the chemo won't work? Is there any real medical data to support that line of reasoning?"

"We know what works," he insisted, looking at the other patients nervously. "And besides, your insurance company will only pay for a PET scan every three months."

There it was! Even the most well-intentioned treatment recommendations are, to some extent, impacted by economic reality.

"You need to complete the program," the doctor said.

Now I found myself in a real dilemma. Should I force his hand and insist on the scan? Should I walk out of the room? *I just want to go home!*

With tears filling my eyes, I heard God's voice: "You trust me. I rescue you. You glorify me."

"OK," I said. "I'll have the infusion today."

The silence of the room rang in my ears. No one had anything to say. I finished the day crying and praying—a quivering mass of nerves—a mere shadow of the man who had walked confidently into the Tiki Room nine weeks earlier. What did they think of me now?

Week Ten

My physical and emotional conditions had once again deteriorated beyond description. In particular, the rash on my face was spreading faster than a computer virus. Small whiteheads across the bridge of my nose and forehead burst and bled at the slightest touch. I had to cover my pillow each night to protect it from the matter oozing from my infected pores.

My wife tried to be the best encouragement she could be. Friends and relatives called daily to reassure me they were praying and would continue to pray. Many offered to stop by as they had so often during the past few weeks. At this point, however, visitors were an unwelcome thought. I couldn't stand the sight of myself in the mirror—I certainly was not going to subject anyone else to the spectacle.

Egg-white omelets with kale and arugula were really getting old. Spoonfuls of molasses were anything but tasty. I'd lost count of the pills I took every day in an attempt to suppress the chemo side effects. Moving from the bed to the bathroom and back to the bed occupied most of my daily routine. The sight of my spindly arms and legs would have been funny if not so pathetic.

Nicole was shocked at the extent of the rash on my face and hesitant to insert the acupuncture needles into my forehead for fear of aggravating the condition. After strategically placing several into my ankles, she applied fragrant oil to her hands and began to rub my aching feet. My only response was a series of soft moans. She listed the various internal organs impacted by pressure applied to various points on my soles. She was heaven-sent. Maybe I could get through this after all.

I returned to the center on July 18 for my tenth infusion. Could I do it? Maybe I could. The psychological effect of knowing there were only two infusions remaining gave me courage.

Dr. Chen could not believe the severity of my reaction to the Erbitux. "Your face is really inflamed," he proclaimed. "I'm going to prescribe an antibiotic to keep it from becoming infected."

The premeds were administered, and the adjusted steroid dosage was soon overpowered by the Benadryl. The resulting drowsiness actually allowed me to sleep during most of the infusion. Before I realized it, the hours had passed.

"We're all through, Mr. Craig," the nurse announced. "We'll see you next week."

Well, maybe you will and maybe you won't.

Only hours after the infusion, my face began to swell. I was positive it was the cumulative effects of the Erbitux. It was hard to find a comfortable position for sleeping. I took several milligrams of a natural sleeping agent just to get some much-needed rest. When

I awakened, my eyes were swollen shut and my face looked like I had fallen asleep under a sun lamp. The swelling produced a lot of pain. I was understandably upset. It hurt!

After two days of indescribable misery, my wife called the center and explained our situation. Dr. Chen wanted to see me immediately. My wife had to drive because I was unable to see through the tiny slits where my eyes were supposed to be.

"In all my experience I've never seen a reaction to Erbitux this bad," he told us. "I'm going to prescribe a special ointment to keep your skin moist. Also, I'm afraid we won't be able to give you your next infusion. We need to give you a break from the chemo."

Finally! Something good had come of all this!

When we got home, I applied the ointment to my face and climbed into bed. I was able to get to sleep quickly. At two in the morning I awoke with a jolt. My face felt like it was going to burst apart. The severity of the swelling had caused my skin to crack in multiple places, and blood was running down my face.

My emotions took over. I was sobbing and crying—deep, hurting, uncontrollable weeping. Cold water provided some temporary relief from the burning pain. My wife was at my side, trying to calm me and apply the antibiotic ointment.

"It hurts, it hurts!" I screamed.

"I know—I'm so sorry!"

"I'm not doing this anymore! I can't do this anymore! I won't go back! I'm through! I can't believe God really expects me to torture myself this way!

"OK, OK. We'll talk about it later."

WEEK ELEVEN

Within a few days the facial swelling began to decrease. The cracked skin began to dry up and flake off. For several weeks I literally peeled layer after layer of skin from my face. The exposed nerve endings required constant attention to prevent infection and provide some pain relief.

Having two weeks with no chemotherapy brought a welcome respite to my psyche and an opportunity for my body to heal. Believing I wouldn't have to do this to myself again provided a boost to my emotional state. While full recovery would be six months away, I knew I was on its path.

On July 31 we received a call from SCTWC reminding me of my infusion appointment on August 1.

"I won't be there," I told the receptionist.

"Really? It says here you've only had ten of the twelve scheduled infusions."

"I know, but I'm done."

"OK. I'll let the doctor know."

A few minutes later the phone rang again. "This is Dr. Chen. The receptionist tells me you're not coming in for your infusion tomorrow."

"That's right. In two weeks I'll be eligible for another PET scan. I'll discuss the results with Dr. Seely and then decide what the next step will be. Remember, my plan was to use the chemotherapy to shrink the tumor so I could have the rest of it surgically removed."

"Mr. Craig, I know this has been hard on you, but you really need to complete what you started if you want the surgery to be successful. Please come in tomorrow so we can at least talk about it."

This guy just won't give up! I'm feeling a little better after my two-week break. I guess it can't hurt to at least talk to him. Sigh. "OK. I'll see you tomorrow."

I hung up the phone and heard that voice in the back of my head saying, "You need to trust me—I will rescue you, so you can give me the glory."

Chapter Nine

WORKING OUT

RIGHT DECISIONS

"Trust in the Lord with all your heart;
do not depend on your own understanding.
Seek his will in all you do, and he will show you
which path to take."
—Proverbs 3:5-6 NLT

I WASN'T SURPRISED at the looks I received as I hobbled into the clinic. The organization was small enough that most of the staff knew the details of many patient cases.

I weighed 160 pounds—fifteen pounds less than when I began ten weeks before. As expected, my blood pressure was higher than normal—my emotions more tattered than a pair of fashionable jeans.

I followed Dr. Chen to a private room. He attempted to persuade me that this treatment regimen was the proven one. His words did little to encourage me to have another infusion. Then it hit—I began using my fingers to make certain I'd counted correctly—this was actually week twelve! Even though I'd received only ten infusions, this was still the twelfth week. Completing one more infusion would mean completing twelve weeks. With that simple psychological mind trick, I convinced myself I could do it.

"Great," said the doctor. "I'll write the prescription. What made you change your mind?"

"Knowing this is the last time I'll have to do this."

"What? No. You need to come back next week for one more infusion."

"But this is the twelfth week," I reminded him.

"Yes, but it's only your eleventh infusion," he argued.

Right or wrong, that was the last time I saw Dr. Chen in 2007. I made a decision that day not to have any more chemotherapy. Despite calls from the center during the coming days, reminding me of my final appointment, I assured them I had completed my mission. That's called patient power.

Anxious to know the results of the chemo regimen, I called Dr. Seely's office and ordered a PET scan. My old friends at Washington Imaging were horrified at my appearance. A smattering of white stubble on my head, my face inflamed and scarred, and my frame small and frail—I looked like Yoda! (Of these things, much more we will speak.)

I visited Dr. Seely on August 16 to review the scans. "The chemo definitely had an effect on the tumor," he said. The scan report included these statements:

Dramatic *decrease* in size of a region of squamous cell carcinoma.

Dramatic *decrease* in the size of … lymph node medial to the left … consistent with a dramatic response to chemotherapy.

Interval *decrease* in the degree of enhancement and posterior triangular lymph nodes in lower left neck consistent with a response to chemotherapy.

No new or enlarging lymph nodes are present in the neck.

Additionally, no suspicious activity of any kind could be found in the pelvic region. Dr. Chen was right—I wouldn't need exploratory colon surgery. We finally closed that subject.

This was all wonderful news. Why then did I feel so bad? I knew I was alive, but I didn't feel alive. Something wasn't right. There was unsettledness deep in my soul. Somehow, I knew it wasn't over. Class was still is session.

TIME IS RUNNING OUT

In early September we drove to Arizona. With chemotherapy behind us, we began another recovery process. For five years this had been the story of our lives—treatment, recovery, treatment, recovery, treatment, recovery. All the while we continued to wonder when and how it might all end.

Dr. Seely had sent the PET scans to Paul for review. "It looks like the chemo did its job," Paul said. "It appears we can remove any remaining tissue without as great a risk of damage to the cranial nerves." Terrific! We discussed a date for surgery, probably sometime in mid-October. I would need to prepare myself physically by exercising and gaining as much weight as possible.

"You will most likely have to be on a liquid diet for some time following surgery," Paul explained, "so you'll want to bulk up as much as you can."

Not an easy task for a person with the metabolism of a hummingbird. I'd have to consume six thousand calories a day and pump iron like a member of the World Wrestling Federation! The most I could hope for was to get back the weight I had lost.

A few days later, Paul called to tell me he'd met a colleague at a regional conference. "I was most impressed with him," he said. "Coincidentally, he belongs to the otolaryngology group at the Mayo Clinic in Scottsdale." This head and neck cancer specialist, known for his excellence in the application of transoral micro laser surgery, might be able to provide a second opinion as to whether debulking surgery would be an appropriate next step.

At Paul's suggestion we called the Mayo Clinic and made an appointment to see the surgeon on September 25. As instructed, we forwarded, in advance of the appointment, my complete medical history.

The Mayo Clinic, known worldwide for its research and treatment capabilities, is truly an amazing organization, with comfortable, attractive, and technologically advanced facilities. The surgeon was professional, articulate, and compassionate. He obviously had read every page in my medical file—ten years of cancer-related paperwork. Not a simple task.

After performing his own oral examination, he said, "Yours is an amazing case. I don't think I've encountered anything quite like it."

"We get that a lot," I replied, smiling at my wife.

"You are a fortunate individual. However, I'm afraid time might be running out for you. We need to take immediate action to get rid of this thing."

The smiles left our faces. What action? I had just finished three months of chemotherapy and had not yet recovered. Did he not see the stubble on my head and my ruddy complexion? We tried to explain our intent to have debulking surgery in October.

"I don't think that's such a great idea," he said. "I'm generally the first person to suggest surgery—ask anyone in the clinic. However, there is too much abnormal tissue to attempt such a feat. Not even with the use of a laser."

What else was there, if surgery was not an option?

"My highest recommendation" he continued, "is that you have radiation—and that you have it as soon as possible. I can arrange for you to meet with our best radiation oncologist to start the process as soon as next week." He told us of his shock to read that I had refused radiation in 1997 and again in 2003.

I guess we asked for it. We wanted a second opinion, and we got it.

"We have a strong faith," I told him. "We believe it is God who has kept the cancer isolated and slow growing. We've also been told by more than one member of our medical team that we have made all the right decisions during the last ten years with regard to treatment—treatment that has controlled the cancer."

"I can appreciate that," he replied. "I just hope you'll make the right decision this time."

Reluctantly, but since this *was* the Mayo Clinic, we agreed to an appointment with the radiation oncologist. Perhaps technology had improved the process sufficiently to avoid some of the incapacitating side effects we'd read and heard so much about.

As we were leaving the examination room, the doctor asked, "Since your case is so unusual, may I have your permission to present it to our multidisciplinary head and neck tumor board for discussion?"

My case being presented to a group of the best minds the Mayo Clinic had to offer? I didn't know whether to be flattered or insulted.

"Why not," I answered.

RADIATION—OUR BEST HOPE?

It was time for more research. If I was going to have an intelligent discussion with a radiation oncologist, I wanted to be armed with as much information on the subject as possible. Thank God for the World Wide Web.

Unfortunately, I was not able to find much more data than I had gleaned from previous investigations. My friend George had shared the results of his own radiation research, and none of it was very appealing. I did learn that radioactive implants could be used in conjunction with surgery. A small, seed-like device is placed into the tumor area and radiation is released over time. I also discovered that partial doses and organ-specific radiation treatments were available.

My research confirmed again the potentially horrific and incapacitating—temporary and permanent—side effects of radiation, including osteoradionecrosis (deterioration of the bone) in the jaw. This was the side effect I feared most.

We traveled to the clinic on September 27 for our appointment with the radiation oncologist. He was younger than we expected but a professional nonetheless. We patiently answered the same questions we'd been asked two days before. This doctor was also astonished that, after ten years, the cancer had not spread beyond a defined area.

"We believe God has intervened in our behalf," we declared.

The doctor nodded politely. "May I examine you?"

His exam included a tongue swipe. Pulling my tongue out of my mouth as far as he could with one hand, he used the forefinger of the other to swipe the back of my tongue, feeling for any tumor or abnormal growth. "This may cause you to gag a little," he warned.

A little? I thought I was going to hack up a lung!

Removing his latex gloves, the doctor solemnly declared, "Radiation is your best hope for survival." He described it as full-dose, full-course, full-field gamma ray bombardment of the tongue, throat, and neck. The radiation would be administered over a period of eight weeks, along with more chemotherapy.

Chemotherapy? That got my attention. "What chemo drugs do you use?"

"Cisplatin."

I still had nightmares about the horrific effects of cisplatin given me in 1997 and 2003. "Why does it have to be a full dose? Why do you want to radiate my entire throat and neck? Why can't we use partial doses and target the tumor specifically?"

"I'm sorry," he said soulfully. "I cannot recommend anything less. You have a window of opportunity here. This may well be your last chance to finally overcome the disease."

He went on to describe the side effects. Nothing we didn't already know, except for one small detail, which he carefully omitted. He did not mention the possibility for bone loss.

"What about osteoradionecrosis?" I chirped.

"Yes. That is always a possibility. In your case it would most likely be a probability. But we have technically advanced reconstruction techniques for rebuilding your jawbone."

At least he hadn't tried to soft sell the program. I almost wished he had.

The next few seconds of silence felt more like hours. I looked at my wife and could see in her eyes the monster of hopelessness rearing its ugly head.

Finally, I said to the doctor, "I'm sorry. I am not physically, mentally, or emotionally prepared to consent to such a radical treatment program at this time."

The brilliance of that warm, sun-filled afternoon went unnoticed as we walked silently back to our car. Once we were on our way, my wife said, "We've heard all that doom and gloom before. What are we going to do now?"

I didn't have any answers. Silently, I wondered if I had made the right choice.

Beyond Our Ability To Cure

I called Paul and told him of our experience with the Mayo Clinic physicians. He was surprised, to say the least. We were both disappointed in the apparent narrow focus of such a prestigious medical group. They seemed unwilling to try different applications of treatment—even at the patient's request.

For the next week or so, we watched the hours drift by like a leaf on a lazy stream—slowly, steadily, inevitably—toward an unknown destination. We tried desperately to shut out thoughts of what might lie ahead, even though we knew God was ultimately in control. It would have been helpful to know what he had in mind—the still waters of confirmation or the turbulent rapids of indecision. Either way, we were in his hands.

After prayerful consideration, we agreed that debulking surgery was the best course of action. Paul requested an operating room at the UAB Medical Center for October 16. His instructions to the scheduling staff read, "Please get Mr. David Craig set up for the following: open right partial laryngectomy, partial glossectomy, and ipsilateral Level I-III neck dissection." In laymen's terms, he was going to remove part of my voice box, most of the base of my tongue, and the lymph nodes in the right side of my neck—at the very least.

A week before our departure for Alabama, we received a letter from the Mayo Clinic. Attached was a two-page memorandum summarizing the results of the discussion of my case by the clinic's head and neck tumor board. The letter read:

Dear Mr. Craig:

Your case was presented to the Multidisciplinary Head and Neck Tumor Board at the Mayo Clinic Arizona on October 2, 2007. Those in attendance included head and neck oncologic surgeons from the Department of Otolaryngology to include your surgeon, as well as physicians from the Radiation Oncology Department and the Medical Oncology Department here at Mayo Clinic.

Your case was discussed in great detail at this meeting. We reviewed your history, your physical examination, your radiographic x-rays, and your pathology. Following the presentation of your case, there was considerable discussion about what your best treatment option would be at this point. It is the unanimous recommendation of the Multidisciplinary Head and Neck Tumor Board at Mayo Clinic Arizona, that you be treated with a full course of radiotherapy, to include a full dose of radiotherapy to your base of tongue, as well as to the neck and surrounding tissues. We would recommend against any therapy which would fall short of this, to include partial doses of radiation therapy or radiation therapy to only the tongue base or the neck. This recommendation is based on the fact that to date you continue to have evidence of squamous cell carcinoma that, though it has had a good tumor biology thus far, is likely to eventually alter in its tumor biology and become more aggressive, at which point it may be beyond our ability to cure your cancer.

"... beyond our ability to cure your cancer." That was the phrase that surprised and confused me the most. All of my research told me (and still tells me) that cancer is an incurable disease. I understand that certain cancers can be eradicated. I know surgery can be successfully used to remove cancerous cells from the body. However, no medication or vaccine is currently available to provide immunity from cancer or to ensure the disease will never return. If it is curable, why do I still receive mail from various foundations soliciting donations to help find a cure for cancer? At best, current treatment methods seem only to keep the disease in remission.

With that in mind, why does the medical community at large continue to apply treatment methods with the goal of curing an incurable disease, particularly when too many patients succumb to the treatment itself?

The Mayo Clinic head and neck tumor board admitted that the biology of my tumor was unlike that generally characteristic of squamous cell carcinoma. I was therefore convinced that my approach to cancer as a chronic disease, and not a terminal illness, was the correct approach for me. All of my efforts were centered on the control or management of the disease, with the goal of retaining as much capacity and quality of life as possible. Making a decision to accept full-course, full-dose, full-field radiation, with its incapacitating side effects, did not meet that goal. It was not that the Mayo Clinic had an uncaring attitude, or that their recommendation wasn't correct (given their treatment philosophy). It was simply not the right treatment recommendation for me.

In the last ten years I have observed that the control or management approach to cancer is not one most oncologists or surgeons will recommend—even those who are proponents of patient empowerment. Sadly, academic disciplines, by-the-book training, liability insurance underwriters, and (often) economics prevent professional, intelligent, well-meaning practitioners from thinking outside the medical box.

God showed his favor by directing me to physicians like Daniel Seely and Paul Castellanos, men unafraid to step outside the invisible boundaries created by the certificates and diplomas hanging on their office walls. They respected my decisions without applying undo pressure or influence by using the letters that follow their names.

Believe it or not, the doctor doesn't always know best just because he's the doctor, and no recommendation is the right one if the patient is not comfortable with it.

LIFE LIKE QUICKSAND

We traveled to Birmingham on Saturday, October 13, 2007, and checked into the familiar surroundings of the Courtyard Marriott. On Sunday we attended church with Paul and his family and were invited to their home for a leisurely afternoon visit. We talked about our children, the weather, politics, movies, and life in general. It was a welcome break.

On Monday I walked to the medical complex for pre-op testing and evaluation. After a blood draw to ensure a match for a potential transfusion during surgery, all systems were go for the operation, and we spent the evening in quiet contemplation of the coming events. Alone with my thoughts, I questioned again whether this was the right course of action.

On Tuesday morning I was admitted for surgery. Carolyn's e-mail updates describe what happened over the next couple of days:

October 16, 2007, 12:00 P.M.

I'm trying to keep my mind busy. Can't seem to settle down ... We had to be in admitting at six this morning ... they took David back for prep at six-thirty. I didn't get to see him for over an hour. We had about fifteen minutes together before they wheeled him away. He was having a harder time than usual ... very pensive and nervous (that would be normal for me, but usually not for him). I think we both realize this might be his last treatment option. It is very hard when he leaves ... the hours seem endless.

It will probably be six to eight hours (before I see him again) so I will continue to go back and forth between the waiting room and our hotel room. Thank goodness they have a Starbucks just outside the waiting area.

The doctor had the surgical nurse call me in the waiting area around ten-thirty to say things were going well ... he was stable. They'll check with me periodically ... I leave after each update and return an hour or so later.

Thank you all for your love and concern ... a special thanks to those of you who have called to pray with me or just to chat and let me know your thoughts and prayers are with us. All of this helps the hours slip by.

I was just getting ready to send this e-mail when my cell phone rang ... it was a nurse from a doctor's office in Washington. I had mentioned the date of David's surgery ... she had written it on their calendar and was calling to check in. How wonderful to know that so many people take on our burden and remember us in prayer. This has been so touching to me. God has placed wonderful people in my life.

October 16, 2007, 7:30 P.M.

It has been a very long day. We started at six this morning and David was in surgery until six tonight. They explored his throat with a scope and started surgery a little before nine. I talked to the doctor around five-forty-five ... the team was just finishing up with him. Paul believes he got 95 percent of the tumor. He suggested that David follow up with chemo (he won't like that) ... it would be somewhere down the road, as it will be months before he gets his strength back and recovers from surgery. They will keep a breathing tube in his throat at least until tomorrow. He has a feeding tube running through his nose to his stomach ... only time will determine when it can come out ... it will depend upon how well he responds and whether or not he will (ultimately) have to have a feeding tube in his stomach. He has shocked doctors and therapists in the past so I'm expecting him to do so again.

The surgery took so long because of its delicate nature. The doctor was able to save two out of three of those important cranial nerves. The third he believes has been destroyed ... there was so much scar tissue it was difficult to say for sure. I asked him if he could see the tumor ... he said he went by "feel." We are so blessed to have found Paul as our surgeon. He and our doctor in Washington have been the only physicians willing to listen to David's wishes for controlling, rather than attempting to cure the disease.

I still haven't been able to see David yet. He is in ICU ... they are very strict about visitors. I'm going to call and make one more trip over to the hospital. He won't know I'm there but just need to touch him and see him for myself.

Has this been hard? Oh, for sure!!!!!! Have we been down? Well, you bet!!!!!! Has God has his hand on our lives and seen us through? Without a doubt!!!!!!!!!

October 17, 2007, 11:30 A.M.

Things are going well but not without a few glitches.

They removed the breathing tube this morning ... much earlier than expected. David is sitting up but still connected to all kinds of tubes and wires. They have removed his wrist restraints since he is doing so well on the pain meds ... he is not agitated like he was [last year] when he was on morphine. They aren't concerned that he will yank things out this time. Miraculously, he HAS HIS VOICE ... this has always been a concern. We feel so blessed! However, he is on total voice rest and will be for some time. He is not to attempt to use his voice for any reason.

The doctor called me a short while ago and said that the two drains in David's neck were not working correctly. He wanted to warn me not to be shocked when I see David later ... he had to be bound with material around his throat and neck to compress the wound made by the incision. Paul believes a pinhole leak has occurred. If the compress doesn't correct the problem, he'll have to perform an exploratory procedure in the next day or so. Please put this on your prayer list. This could really set things back. He said David isn't very happy ... it was nice he warned me. In the grand scheme of things, this is a minor problem ... so I won't let him go into a self-pity mode. I'm sure it isn't comfortable for him at all ... he's very emotional anyway.

We never know how deep we can dig inside ourselves until put to the test. Sometimes life feels like quicksand ... but with God on our side we eventually, and always, reach solid ground.

WHY DID I DO THIS?

The binding around my neck was extremely restrictive. I tried to communicate my discomfort, but apparently the nursing staff couldn't grasp the meaning of my hand gestures. (Well, they finally understood one of them. Unfortunately, that didn't make my stock go up.) I've never been a very good patient. Have I mentioned that before?

My breathing sounded like air escaping from a damaged bicycle tire. Paul visited me to investigate the leak in my airway. He inserted a long, thin, flexible tube up and through my right nasal passage and snaked it down into the back of my throat.

"Ah ha!" he exclaimed to the resident assisting him. "I see the problem. We'll have to operate again. Schedule him for surgery."

"I'm sorry, buddy," he said. "I promise it won't take long."

Later that afternoon I was wheeled into the operating room with no pre-op ceremonies. A team of five strangers hurriedly prepared me for surgery. One team member attempted to start an IV. "I can't seem to find a vein," she said. "Hold on, Mr. Craig, I'm trying to give you some I-don't-care medicine." She missed the vein again, prolonging the painful process. Finally, as blood ran down my arm, the medicine was administered and I slowly drifted into unconsciousness. Carolyn's e-mail tells the rest of the story:

October 19, 2007, 8:00 P.M.

Last night the doctor did a clean-up surgery on David and fixed the airway leak. It was a short surgery but seemed like another long wait. The waiting room was empty except for three women waiting to see their loved one. Seeing I was alone ... and true to their Southern hospitality, they have taken me under their wings. Now we meet at visiting time and they insist I have meals with them. It has been nice to have someone to talk to besides doctors and nurses.

We waited most of the day for David to get moved from ICU to step-down. I was allowed in ICU only during visiting hours.

Finally, around two-thirty they let me stay with him until he was moved and settled. They started giving him some ice chips to suck on ... he choked ... he was very discouraged. Later in the afternoon he was able to take a few sips of water. The doctor and his assistant were in disbelief.

I was still on voice rest when the doctor congratulated me on my ability to take a few sips of water. "That's great, buddy," he said. "In a couple of days, we'll do a swallowing test to see whether you need a G-tube." A G-tube; the one post-surgical device I feared the most. My expression told him of my displeasure.

"I've got good news," he continued. "Your pathology report came back today."

"You mean you got clear margins around the tumor?" I whispered.

"Clear margins? We weren't even looking for clear margins. There was no cancer found in any of the tissue I removed from your throat!" he stated proudly.

"What do you mean?" I asked. "What method did you use to determine which tissue was cancerous and which was not?"

"I used my eyes," he responded. "I removed any tissue that appeared abnormal. It looks like you had a complete response to the chemotherapy."

Tears began filling my eyes—tears of anger! "If I had a complete response to chemotherapy," I whispered, "why then did I put myself through this mutilating, painful, possibly incapacitating surgery? For ten years I've made all of the right choices for treatment, and now I've made the wrong one?"

Paul began to laugh. "You didn't make the wrong decision," he chided. He attempted to explain the medical reasons why surgery was a good choice. Only the part about cancer being unable to return to tissue that was no longer in my body made any sense. Overcome with emotion, I sobbed uncontrollably. *Dear God, why could you let something like this happen to me? I could have been cancer-free and kept the muscles I needed for swallowing. There is an incision twelve inches long in my neck. I'm missing two-thirds of the muscles and tissue in my throat. What am I going to do now? Maybe*

I should have listened to the Mayo Clinic tumor board and had the radiation! Thoughts invoked by that fiend called self-pity.

When afternoon visiting hours started, Carolyn arrived and dutifully sat by my bedside. She told me of her conversations with the doctor concerning the extent and results of surgery.

"Isn't it wonderful," she exclaimed. "No malignancy found in the tissue!"

"Yeah, wonderful," I replied sarcastically. "I can't believe I put myself through all of this just to find out I had a complete response to chemotherapy."

"Quiet. Remember, you're supposed to rest your voice."

That Could Be Me

My mental state was even more negatively affected by the dysfunctional effects of so much tissue and muscle loss:

The glands in my mouth began to produce excessive saliva, which caused choking and coughing as it overflowed into my airway, requiring the use of a portable suction device.

My tongue, with no supporting foundation, was difficult to control, and as a result I could not articulate certain sounds. The repositioning of my voice box also lowered the resonance of the sounds I could make.

Four of the six muscles that run under the chin and into the neck had been removed. These muscles are crucial to the swallowing process—particularly if food is not chewed into very small pieces.

The final blow came when I saw myself in the bathroom mirror and found a tablespoon-sized hole in the side of my neck. Not only was I functionality impaired, but I was also disfigured.

What good could possibly come from all of this? I was feeling desperately sorry for myself, questioning again my decision to have the surgery.

Being in the step-down ward wasn't much different from being in the ICU. The interval between checks of my vital signs might have been slightly longer, giving me a little more opportunity to sleep. Otherwise, the only significant change was a new team of nurses, all having to learn my specific requirements for care.

During my first night, a young nurse was assigned the task of administering my liquid Tylenol. Since I could not swallow, a large syringe pushed liquids through the feeding tube running up into my left sinus passage and back down into my stomach. On this particular occasion, the nurse failed to lock the syringe firmly onto the end of the feeding tube. When she pushed the plunger, the tube came loose and the bright red liquid splashed onto my face, clothing, and bedding. While I didn't get the Tylenol, I did get a sponge bath, a fresh hospital gown, clean bedding, and a new nurse.

Early the next morning a man was wheeled into the room and settled behind the curtain that separated us. As he was moved passed my bed, I noticed a large device around his neck and bandages wrapped around his head. After his attendants left the room, the only sound I could hear was the gentle pulsing of equipment used to help him breathe.

When visiting hours began, Carolyn came in, conversing with a woman who turned out to be the wife of my new roommate.

"Were you able to get a good night's rest?" she asked.

"In a hospital?" I squeaked. I told her the story of the night nurse trying to drown me in liquid Tylenol.

Sensing my agitation, aggravation, and exasperation, she quickly took control of the conversation. "Did you see the woman I came in with? I met her in the hallway. We had quite a discussion." She proceeded to tell me that the woman's husband had the same base-of-tongue cancer I had. Based upon his doctor's recommendations, he had consented to the traditional chemotherapy and radiation treatments. Predictably, the radiation destroyed the bone in his jaw, and he had been sent from Florida to the University of Alabama for reconstructive surgery. It was yet unknown whether the operation was a success.

His wife informed us that without the use of his jaw, he could not eat or speak. He would have to use a tracheal device for breathing and a G-tube for eating. It was not known for how long he would have to rely upon these devices for function.

After listening to my roommate's story, I became quiet, pensive, and ashamed of myself. Perhaps I had made the right decision after all. With tears in my eyes, I said to my wife, "My God, that could be me."

Later that day I opened the Book for the first time since being hospitalized. Not by coincidence did it fall open at its center. My gaze fell upon the longest chapter in the psalms—Psalm 119. I resolved to read the entire chapter. I read verses like these (italics added):

"How can a young man keep his way pure? By living according to your *word*" (v. 9).

"I have hidden your *word* in my heart that I might not sin against you" (v. 11).

"Do not snatch the *word* of truth from my mouth.... I will speak of your statutes before kings" (vv. 43, 46).

On the napkin from my bed tray, I quickly penned my thoughts—thoughts spoken into my heart by God: "The formula for Working Out Right(eous) Decisions can only be found in God's WORD."

Immediately I recalled John 1:1: "In the beginning was the Word, and the Word was with God, and the Word was God." This verse provided the first element of the formula. The three phrases I read from Psalm 119 provided the rest. Feverishly, I continued to write:

KNOW the Word—John 1:1
HIDE the Word—Psalm 119:11
OBEY the Word—Psalm 119:9
SHARE the Word—Psalm 119:43, 46

All four parts of this formula would become crucial to my understanding of the purposes God had for my situation, as well as for learning the lessons he was teaching me. I was certain I knew the Word—I had a personal relationship with Jesus Christ. I was not as certain I had studied God's Word to the extent he intended. My mind told me I had obeyed God's Word, but my heart told me otherwise. It would become clear that God's plan for me was to share my story and his Word with those who would hear it.

Tearfully, I prayed, "Dear Lord, forgive my whining and complaining. Forgive me for questioning your concern for me and your involvement in my life. You have always been there with just the right answer at just the right time. Thank you for speaking into my heart the words I so desperately needed to hear."

I tucked the napkin safely away. I couldn't wait to tell Carolyn of my encounter with the Creator of the universe. No matter what the days would bring, I had the formula for working out right decisions. All I had to do was put the formula to work in my life.

Chapter Ten

IT'S OK TO FAIL THE TEST

"Then the LORD answered Job from the whirlwind:
'Who is this that questions my wisdom with
such ignorant words?
Brace yourself, because I have some questions for you,
and you must answer them.'"

—Job 38:1-2 NLT

DID YOU KNOW that forty-three separate muscles and nerves must work together, in precisely the correct order, every time you swallow? During this largely unconscious process that takes only a second or two, food is first manipulated by the tongue into the back of the throat. Almost simultaneously, the nasal passages are closed and the voice box begins to move out of the way. As the food moves down the throat, the airway to the lungs closes off so the food can pass by. Finally, the food is pulled down through the esophagus and into the stomach.

Failure of any of these related muscles or nerves to work properly or precisely throughout the swallowing process can result in choking, sucking food into the nasal passages, or entering the airway, causing suffocation. No wonder the psalmist wrote, "I praise you because I am fearfully and wonderfully made; your works are wonderful, I know that full well" (Psa. 139:14).

A day or so later, I was moved into the hospital's general population. Around mid-afternoon, a therapist from the university's speech and swallowing department came by to describe the procedure for my swallowing test. Along with all the devices attached to my body, I was wheeled to a room full of high-tech equipment and instructed to sit on an apparatus resembling a tall, straight-backed chair. As I attempted to swallow foods of varying consistencies spooned into my mouth by the therapist, a technician monitored the process using X-ray equipment.

All of this sounds relatively simple until you consider that I was holding in my lap a five-pound battery pack powering my heart and pulse monitors; I was trying desperately to maintain a modicum of modesty while wearing nothing but a hospital gown tied at the neck; I was fighting back tears at the pulling of the bladder catheter dangling between my legs; and I was shivering violently in a temperature-controlled room. Other than that, it was a piece of cake. Come to think of it, they didn't give me cake—just pudding and juice!

I did not hesitate to alert the four—that's right, four—female attendants conducting the test to my displeasure at having to endure such a humiliating experience. In a very slow, Southern manner, one of them replied, "Don't worry, honey. We've seen it all before."

Of course you have! But you've never seen mine before!

After sixty minutes of this humiliating ordeal, I was returned to my room, muttering my discontent to anyone who would listen. My disposition was made worse by a report from the swallowing therapist that I had failed the test.

Paul visited me during his evening rounds. He was disappointed I had not passed the swallowing test but promised to give me another chance. If I failed a second time, I would be fitted for a G-tube. I was determined not to let that happen. I practiced swallowing using liquids, Jell-O, and thick juices. Having lost almost two-thirds of the muscles used for the process, I had to learn to swallow all over again.

Over the next couple of days, my oxygen line, bladder catheter, and the device inserted under my skin to monitor vital signs came out. Only the IV in my hand, the feeding tube in my nose, and the drainage tube in my neck remained. The freedom to move about was mentally and emotionally uplifting. I was finally able to sleep for more than forty minutes at a time.

With a renewed sense of hope, I faithfully read God's Word, and committed to hiding it in my heart. As I questioned over and over whether I might be able to pass the swallowing test and avoid the G-tube, I resolved again to trust God to do whatever it was he was going to do. He had proven himself with miracle upon miracle.

I began to recover faster than anyone expected. Although a laborious task, I was eating soft foods and articulating, to the amazement of everyone associated with my case. The feeding tube was removed from my nose when I proved I could swallow medications with water. Paul shook his head in disbelief as he watched me move my tongue to the roof and sides of my mouth.

"The residents assisting me in surgery cannot believe you are able to speak or eat so quickly," Paul said. "They saw how much tissue I removed. Few have ever recovered so quickly after losing that much mass. I'm sure you'll have no trouble passing the swallowing test."

"We have a big God," I replied.

"Yes, we do," he agreed.

Paul's prediction was correct. I had no trouble passing the swallowing test. That's not to say I didn't have certain complications; nevertheless, they were deemed minor enough to allow function and avoid the G-tube. God had rescued me—just as he promised.

LONG, SLOW RECOVERY

On October 22, Paul removed the drainage tube—the last foreign object attached to my body. Carolyn took me for a stroll around the hospital ward, and I greeted the nurses who had faithfully attended me. None of them could believe I might be discharged the next day.

We remained in our hotel for several more days for a final exam before going back to Arizona. Paul could do nothing but smile as he viewed the progress of healing in my throat and neck. With a final set of instructions to "take very small bites of food, chew thoroughly, and don't talk with your mouth full," I was sent home to continue the long process of recovery.

Carolyn's e-mail updates:

October 29, 2007

Just wanted you to know we got home safely and David handled the trip quite well. He wore a face mask during the flight and didn't try to eat or drink anything on the plane. He tried to talk (too much) to our friends who picked us up from the airport. Realizing this was the wrong thing to do ... he is now much more quiet and can only speak for short periods of time. I'm feeding him small amounts every three hours or so to keep his weight up. Nothing wrong with his appetite!

Once again, we are so grateful to God for putting all of you in our lives and for the guidance he has given us for David's treatment.

November 03, 2007

Well, here we are in the early morning hours. David is getting lots of rest now and waking less during the night with choking, etc. I'll be glad when my body clock gets regulated.

David has been very discouraged and depressed these past few days. Things are not moving as quickly as he thought they should. Now, that shouldn't surprise anyone [who knows him]. He still has an overabundance of salivary secretion and is constantly coughing and spitting ... his voice doesn't hold out for very long. A couple of days he spent most of the time in bed ... occasionally he'll sit outside for a while and then watch TV. He's not comfortable enough to go out in public—constantly having to clear his throat and cough into a tissue.

The house is very quiet. I forget sometimes he can't speak easily and often talk to him in statements that require an answer. Not a good move. He's been through a lot and has made such good process so quickly ... I think he was expecting things to move much faster. He kept saying to me in the hospital, "What is God trying to teach me this time?" *Could it be patience???* I ask myself. He's always been one that gets bored so easily ... not much he can do about that at this point except to ... learn to be content.

I'm trying different recipes to give him a variety of soft foods. So far, it seems to be successful but we never know what might cause him to choke. He is still learning and trying various swallowing techniques. One day he'll do fine with certain food and the next day have a problem with the same food. He still can't eat any meat unless I mince it into very small bites. It's kind of like moving ... from baby food to junior food ...

Fortunately, this too shall pass! We'll be glad when it is all a distant memory ... it could have been much worse. We thank you all for your continued prayers.

In late November I returned alone to Alabama for my first post-surgical exam. I arrived in the late afternoon, and Paul's wife and kids picked me up at the airport. We met Paul at their home and went to the Cheesecake Factory for dinner. Paul was amazed as he watched the way I was able to consume my meal.

"Just yesterday I was telling one of my colleagues about your case," he said. "His first question was, 'How is he doing with his G-tube?' When I told him you'd never had one, he could not believe it. He was even more amazed when he learned the details of your ten-year battle."

I spent the night with Paul and his family. The next morning we drove to the medical center for my exam. Paul told me that my throat and neck were healing nicely but cautioned that I must take things slowly. "Recovery can be a long, slow process," he said.

"Don't be discouraged if it takes a year or more to regain your strength and capacity. Even then, you may never be able to function the way you did before."

Carolyn's e-mail:

November 29, 2007

David has returned from Alabama with rave reviews. He still has a lot of excess salivary function that might be a permanent condition. Sometimes it is worse than others. He is looking into medications that might temporarily dry it up.

Once again, the doctors are intrigued, as they have never seen a case like his before. We have indeed been blessed to have two doctors that have worked so well together to provide what the patient requests and not let their egos get in the way.

Every time we think of the alternatives that have been offered along the way, we're so thankful we have been led in the right path to preserve his quality of life. Through it all we have been blessed. Hopefully we will one day know the reasons for this long journey ... even if it is just to have carved out new paths for others to try.

I'm hoping this is the last medical update I have to send for a long time to come!!

BECAUSE I SAID SO

Recovery from chemotherapy and surgery has left me with a lot of time on my hands. Restricted to little physical activity, I spend most of my days reading, watching television, and using the computer to journal my experiences. While eating has become easier, the task still leaves me physically drained. I will never again be able to swallow normally. Speaking more than a few sentences at a time produces severe secretion in my throat, and I begin to cough and choke. By mid-afternoon I'm exhausted and ready for a nap. Following an evening meal, I'm ready for bed. *Normal* has been redefined as it applies to our lives.

For several weeks after surgery, I found myself in a cycle of deep depression—questioning again my judgment for having consented to surgery and wondering how many more lessons God might be trying to teach me. On one particularly beautiful, sunny afternoon in March, I opened the Book, trying somehow to make perfect sense of it all. As my mind wandered through the peaks and valleys of the last ten years, I recalled the story of a biblical character named Job. Job had gone through difficult times (having lost everything but his life and his wife) and had questions about his circumstances too. I decided to read the story again.

After thirty-seven chapters of Job's wondering, whimpering, and ultimately whining about his circumstances, God had finally had enough. The Bible says God challenged Job with sixty-six questions—questions on subjects like physics, chemistry, anatomy, zoology, biology, meteorology, and astronomy. Sadly, Job could not answer even one question correctly. He failed the test. Nevertheless, Job learned the lesson.

When my two younger brothers and I were kids, we lived in a small farming community in Southern Idaho. Running behind our house was an irrigation ditch used for watering the lawn. It filled once a week and flooded the grass through a gate opened and closed by my father. The ditch remained full for a day or so after the lawn was watered, and my brothers and I were convinced this three-foot-deep, fast-moving stream could provide welcome relief from the summer heat.

One day as we removed our T-shirts and blue jeans and headed for the water, Mom yelled from the back porch, "Don't even think about jumping into that ditch!"

"Why not? Why can't we? It's hot!"

"Because I said so!" she hollered back.

That wasn't a reason. We needed something more substantial than "because I said so."

Mom loved us very much. She had our best interests at heart and knew what was best for us. She did not believe it necessary to explain herself every time she told us—or asked us—to do something. She simply wanted us to trust her judgment and obey her instructions. Mom knew that the water flowing through that ditch carried unwanted diseases, critters, and sharp debris. It was only good for one thing—watering the grass.

God loved Job very much. Because he had created him, God knew Job better than Job knew himself. God knew what was best for him and had Job's best interests at heart. God did not feel the need to explain everything to Job just because Job needed an explanation. Hence, the test—sixty-six questions Job could not answer. The lesson—"Trust me, just because I said so! I am God and you are not; I really do know what I'm doing."

After miserably failing his test, Job quickly changed his tone. He said, in essence, "I thought I knew everything I needed to know about you, God. Now I've seen your power for myself. I've learned the lessons you've been trying to teach me and will apply them to the rest of my life."

After reading Job's story one more time, I finally realized that it's OK to fail the tests that come with the experiences of life—as long as we learn their lessons.

In April 2008 I returned to Birmingham for a PET scan and a second post-surgical examination. I arrived the day before the scheduled exams and spent the night with Paul and his family.

On the drive to the medical center the next morning, I recited my list of recovery issues: fatigue and general malaise; constant secretion in my throat resulting in coughing and expectorating; the inability to position my tongue for articulation of certain sounds; the slow, labored process of eating; constant ringing in my ears; my inability to distinguish and understand certain tonal sounds; problems with concentration and recall; and my overall frustration for having elected surgery in the first place.

After listening to my list of complaints, Paul began to laugh.

"What's so funny?"

Without hesitation he said, "I have no less than a hundred patients who've gone through a similar scale of surgery. Every one of them would give an arm to be able to have your degree of functionality."

"That would make the old saying true. 'No matter how bad we believe our situation to be, there is always someone worse off than we are.'"

Paul performed an extensive laryngoscopy, recording the exam on video for future reference. He saw a couple of things that concerned him. "Your upper esophagus sphincter muscle is swollen, and you have a sliding hiatal hernia," he declared. "I want to perform a swallowing test. Let's give the anesthetic about an hour to wear off, and we'll see what's happening in your throat."

I sat in the waiting area as instructed, wondering what I might be facing next. After thirty minutes or so, a tall, middle-aged man with a large bandana wrapped around his neck checked in at the appointment desk. He was quickly admitted and emerged after only a few minutes. He had a look of despair on his face as he left the clinic.

My name was called, and I was escorted to an examination room where Paul was waiting. He told me that the man with the bandana had been diagnosed with base-of-tongue cancer six months before. "Following his doctors' recommendation, he agreed to full-course, full-dose, full-field radiation with chemotherapy. The radiation was so devastating that his airway is now no larger than the tip of a ballpoint pen. The bandana around his neck covers the tracheal tube that allows him to breathe."

I sat, dazed by Paul's words, as he continued to tell me that this man had been sent to him as a last resort. As a result of the radiation, surgery was not a viable treatment option. Listening to this story left me overwhelmed by the reality of God's power, guidance, and mercy in my life. How could I have ever questioned his methods?

Using another specialized scope, Paul watched closely as I swallowed water, crackers, and pudding.

"I see the problem!" he exclaimed. "The food is not being pulled into your esophagus properly. In fact, some of it is being trapped in the back of your throat." He explained that the swelling in the muscle at the top of my esophagus might be corrected with medication. Additionally, reconstructive surgery should be considered to make the swallowing process somewhat less cumbersome.

More surgery?

We decided to postpone any surgical decision until the fall of 2008 to allow my throat additional time to heal and to see if the esophageal problem might correct itself. Paul reviewed with me the results of my PET scan. As expected, he saw nothing in the scans that would indicate any residual cancer. For the first time since 1998, the disease was officially in remission. I'm finally convinced I made the right decisions after all. God rescued me because I placed my trust in him and him alone. I am alive today for one reason—to share my story with others so God can receive the glory!

WORDS TO LIVE BY

The purpose of any test is to determine whether the individual under examination has learned the lesson implicit in the exam. In the testing process, evidence of lessons learned is found in the choices made by the one being tested. A wrong choice can have devastating results. Not only can it result in failing the test but also in having to learn the lesson the hard way—that is, suffering the consequences of failure—and having to take the test again.

Learning the lesson, however, is only the first step. What happens if a lesson learned is then ignored? What happens if a lesson learned is subsequently forgotten? What happens if we fail to apply the lesson to future circumstances? Ignorance, forgetfulness, or failure to implement knowledge gained from experience can result in having to repeat the entire course in God's classroom of life.

The first five books of the Bible tell of a people group who understood this concept all too well. The nation of Israel, today the centerpiece of world foreign policy and controversy, was tested by God time after time in his effort to teach them the lessons necessary for earthly—as well as eternal—life. He tested them to see if they would trust him, and only him. He tested them to see if they would follow his instructions. He tested them to see if they loved him with all of their hearts.

More than once the Israelites failed the tests related to God's lessons for them. So, instead of making a path directly from Egypt into the land God had promised them, they were detoured around a mountain call Sinai. Even when they did learn a lesson, and promised to never repeat their bad choices, these chosen people often failed to apply to their lives what they had learned. As a result they were doomed to another trip around the mountain—never gaining access to the Promised Land until a generation had passed.

The most significant choices inherent in the tests we experience in life are found in the specific lesson or lessons being taught. However, in every instance the fundamentals are the same. First, God uses every opportunity to reveal himself to us. Second, the motive for this revelation is to engage us in relationship with him. Third, a relationship with God is intended to produce total reliance upon him and obedience to him.

The choices are simple: Acknowledge God as the central figure in your life—or not. Accept his Son Jesus Christ as the Savior of your soul—or not. Allow God's Holy Spirit to take control of your life—or not.

The famous, though sometimes controversial, Swiss theologian Karl Barth was a great thinker, a prolific writer, and a professor at several leading European universities. The story is told of an occasion on which he was confronted by a reporter who wanted a brief summary of his twelve volumes on church dogma. Barth, who could have given an impressive intellectual reply or a profound theological dissertation, instead simply replied, "Jesus loves me this I know, for the Bible tells me so."

Jesus Christ, the often controversial and culture-challenging Son of God, performed many miracles while here on earth and was a profound speaker in many Jewish synagogues. On one occasion a member of a sect called Pharisees came to Jesus in the middle of the night with questions concerning his claims of divinity and messianic purpose. Jesus could have launched into a long theological dissertation concerning the incarnation of God. Instead he softly said, "For God so loved the world that he gave his one and only Son, that whoever believes in him shall not perish but have eternal life" (John 3:16).

AFTER WORDS

"Praise the LORD, I tell myself;
with my whole heart, I will praise his holy name.
Praise the LORD, I tell myself,
and never forget the good things he does for me.
He forgives all my sins
and heals all my diseases.
He ransoms me from death
and surrounds me with love and tender mercies.
He fills my life with good things.
My youth is renewed like the eagles!"
　　　　　　　　　　　　　　—Psalm 103:1-5 NLT

I RETURNED TO Birmingham in December 2008 for another PET scan. For the first time since 1997 no cancer could be found in the right side of my neck or throat. However, a large mass centered in a lymph node on the left side was suspicious for squamous cell carcinoma. After discussing the findings with Paul, we agreed I would return in February 2009 for the surgical removal of the mass and correction of the issues resultant from surgery in 2007.

In light of previous cancer treatments, the surgery was uneventful. Along with the cancerous mass, several other left-side lymph nodes and salivary glands were excised. Pathology confirmed removal of the malignant cells with very clear margins. However, this good news was not without its side effects and several pending issues.

Swallowing is among those issues. Often, if I do not pay close attention to the process, severe choking and coughing ensue. Naturally produced saliva, which is normally swallowed in an unconscious manner, requires conscious throat clearing to prevent choking. This issue makes prolonged speaking extremely difficult. There are residual hot spots on the left side of my tongue base suspicious for cancer recurrence, requiring periodic examination. The hiatal hernia, resultant from chemotherapy, contributes to severe acid reflux when not suppressed with medication. Finally, surgery performed in 2007 and 2009 have left me disfigured on both sides of my neck and throat. Granted, this is a small price to pay for disease control, but is still less than the quality of life I previously enjoyed.

For all intent and purpose, any cancer in my body is currently in remission. Nevertheless, these questions remain: Have I learned all of the lessons God is trying to teach me? If I have, will I ignore them or forget them? Am I willing to apply to my life what I've learned? What other lessons might God have for me? What means will he use to administer future tests? To be certain, no test is valid unless it pushes us beyond the previous test.

The compilation of this manuscript was interrupted by a continuous cycle of medical testing, treatment, recovery side effects, and related issues. Despite these interruptions, I resolved to complete what I had begun in the chemotherapy group room during the spring of 2007—reduce to writing the details of my sojourn with God through these painful events.

However, while the spirit is willing, the body—and the mind—is weak. Twelve years of battling cancer has left many scars, including the inability to concentrate or easily process complex transactions. The synapses of the brain simply do not fire like they did before cancer. The fact that I've been able to write the book you're now reading is a miracle itself. I have medical records, e-mails, and journals supporting all of the facts. Moreover, I've lived out and lived through each set of circumstances. Nonetheless, finding appropriate words and phrases to engage the reader emotionally presented a daunting task. It has been, to say the least, a sentence-by-sentence project, taking more than a year to finish.

This story of what God has done with me, through me, and for me would not be complete without a recap of the most important lessons learned. A comprehensive description of what God wants us to learn is found in the Book: God's Word, the Bible. It is the text for this course of study we call life and contains all of the answers to any test that might come our way. Making a wrong choice is most often the result of failure to open the Book.

God's initial lesson to humanity is that God is God – man is not God; the 'bad things' that happen in life, including disease, serve to remind us of that fact. That said I do not believe God singled me out to remind me of his sovereignty. He did not curse me with cancer for breaking one or more of the Ten Commandments. Did these thoughts cross my mind? Of course – I'm human! But they were only part of the many questions raised out of fear for my life. I believe God used my cancerous situation as an opportunity for me to fall deeper in love with him. After all, fear will drive us to God, but only love will keep us there.

In the paragraphs that follow, I provide the results of the schooling I endured. I hope you learn from my experiences—possibly avoiding a requirement to take the test yourself. If you're already in the midst of a tragedy, wondering where it all might end, perhaps these lessons will apply to your own circumstances.

LESSONS—BY GOD

Lesson 1: Hello, Down There!

Many people foolishly choose to believe the bad things that happen in life are coincidental, happenstance, or ill-fated karma. Doing so, they choose to deny the existence of a higher deity, a divine creator, or a heavenly Father—and many people are in denial. I do not question the fact that human beings often bring problems upon themselves as a result of their own actions. I do question those who refuse to believe that God uses those circumstances to reveal himself.

God said through the psalmist, "The fool says in his heart, 'There is no God'" (Psa. 14:1).

No one will argue that potentially tragic circumstances always get the attention of those involved in the tragedy. For people who have known a relationship with Jesus Christ, such a wake-up call has an even greater impact. I should know.

The question, then, is this: Toward whom or what, is that attention directed? Toward others upon whom we might lay the blame for our plight? Toward an unseen enemy who has it in for us? Or does it result in an acknowledgment that God is more than just a word in our cultural vocabulary?

King David of Israel was not unacquainted with God's methods for getting and keeping his attention. He too had to learn lessons the hard way—and often more than once. He also knew God would never give up on him: "I can never escape from your Spirit! I can never get away from your presence! If I go up to heaven, you are there; if I go down to the grave, you are there.... I cannot hide from you" (Psa. 139:7–8, 12 NLT).

> *God will use whatever it takes,*
> *for as long as it takes, to get and keep our attention.*

Lesson 2: Don't Worry About It!

A most perplexing mystery of the human psyche is the unquenchable thirst to know why. We need an explanation. God, where are you? Why did you let this happen to me? What did I do to deserve this? God, do you really know what you're doing?

When we aren't able to satisfy ourselves with an answer, a seed of suspicion is easily sown in the fertile soil of dismay—not unbelief that God is able to do what he promises but doubt that he actually will. Let's speak plainly: there is a vast difference between honest doubt and flagrant unbelief. Doubt looks for the light; unbelief doesn't want to see the light. Doubt says, I can't believe; unbelief says, I won't believe. Faith, the final goal, brings God pleasure, while doubt arouses his concern. Questions about our circumstances should be a step forward in faith, not the end of faith.

Thankfully, God always responds to doubt with compassion and mercy. When I had doubts that God had healed me of cancer in 2002, he did not slap me around or zap me into oblivion. He used my circumstances to increase my faith, one step at a time, providing all of the tangible evidence I needed.

In the book of Jude, God says, "Be merciful to those who doubt" (v. 22). That means be kind to them, understanding of them, open to their questions, responsive to their pain. If God had not demonstrated all of those characteristics when I was at my lowest point, I would not have the level of faith I have today.

God may not answer all of our questions,
but neither does he condemn our honest doubt.

Lesson 3: Don't Make Me Come Down There!

Making promises or commitments to God in the face of tragedy just to get what we need at the moment can be a costly mistake. Solomon, writing in Ecclesiastes, said, "When you make a promise to God, don't delay in following through, for God takes no pleasure in fools. Keep all the promises you make to him. It is better to say nothing than to make a promise and not keep it. Don't let your mouth make you sin. And don't defend yourself by [saying] that the promise you made was a mistake. That would make God angry, and he might wipe out everything you have achieved" (Eccles. 5:4–6 NLT).

I know all too well the consequences of making promises to God and not keeping them. Promising to change my behavior and then later rationalizing away my sinful actions most assuredly resulted in my having to take this class again. Please understand—God was not trying to destroy me. He simply used the circumstances in my life as an opportunity for me to learn from my mistakes and return to him.

As I write these words, America remembers the lives of loved ones lost in the attacks on the World Trade Center in 2001 and honors the brave men and women who were first on the scene. At the same time, Hurricane Ike is pummeling the coast of Texas at

Galveston, destroying everything in its path. "A tragedy of epic proportion," says Fox News.

How could God allow such devastating events to happen to us? We simply do not wish to believe that a loving heavenly Father might actually allow hurricanes, earthquakes, starvation, disease, terrorism, economic chaos, accidents, or crime to affect the lives of his children. One answer to this dilemma was poignantly offered by Anne Graham Lotz, daughter of evangelist Billy Graham. During an interview with Jane Clayson on the *The Early Show* (CBS) soon after the 9/11 terrorist attacks, Anne said: "I would say also for several years now Americans in a sense have shaken their fist at God and said, 'God, we want you out of our schools, our government, our business, we want you out of our marketplace.' And God, who is a gentleman, has just quietly backed out of our national and political life, our public life—removing his hand of blessing and protection."

God loves us and knows how badly we will hurt ourselves spiritually and physically, if left to our own devices. He wants to have first place in our lives and will do what it takes to make that happen. In the words of the psalmist, "I know, O LORD, that your decisions are fair; you disciplined me because I needed it" (Psa. 119:75 TLT).

I believe God used the cancer in my life to teach me valuable lessons. I know these lessons were right and did me good. How do I know? Not only am I physically alive—my eternal life is secure through my relationship with him.

God expects us to keep the promises we make to him and is willing to chasten us when we don't keep them.

Lesson 4: Would I Lie to You?

We human beings are nothing if not self-sufficient. We can do it all ourselves! Unfortunately, our greatest and weakest tendency is to design our own plans, chart our own course, formulate our own recipe, build our own defense, broker our own investments, plan our own medical treatment, and then ask God to bless what we have done. We have it backwards. "I told you my plans, and you answered. Now teach me your decrees. Help me understand the meaning of your commandments, and I will meditate on your wonderful deeds" (Psa. 119:26–27 NLT).

After trying and failing, the psalmist finally got it right. Realizing his own best-drawn plans would never pass inspection, he tore up the blueprints and asked God to draft a new set.

Each Saturday morning I meet with a group of men to sip coffee and share life experienced throughout the week. Without exception, at least one story includes a reference to a failure to trust God for provision of a need or the consequences reaped from self-laid plans.

Brian faithfully attends our group with his infant son in tow. He vacates the house on Saturday so his wife can sleep in after a week of child care. On one particular occasion I watched in awe as baby Max slept confidently on his father's chest. "Brian," I asked, "how does it feel to know that another human being is totally dependent upon you for everything in his life?"

"It's almost indescribable," he replied. "It is exhilarating, thrilling, exciting, and frightening—all at the same time. There's nothing like it in the whole world!"

"How must God feel," I asked the group, "when we finally reach a place in our lives where we are totally dependent upon him? Why does it often take difficulty, pain, anguish, and even tragedy to help us learn that God simply wants us to rely upon him for everything in our lives—and to trust him to provide it?"

Jesus said, "Come to me, all of you who are weary and carry heavy burdens, and I will give you rest. Take my yoke upon you. Let me teach you, because I am humble and gentle at heart, and you will find rest for your souls. For my yoke is easy to bear, and the burden I give you is light" (Matt. 29:28–30 NLT).

God knows what we need better than we do and wants us to rely totally upon him for everything.

Lesson 5: Remember Me?

As a people we are a throwaway society. If it doesn't work, throw it out. If it looks bad, change it. If it doesn't fulfill expectations, dump it. If it's broken, get rid of it. If it doesn't provide happiness, lose it.

Our cultural landscape is littered with the refuse of unused toys, unwanted jobs, unfulfilled relationships, and unsatisfied souls.

Sadly, we have been influenced by a worldview that teaches that a life once broken somehow cannot have the same value it once had. This secular, progressive philosophy further suggests that opportunity can come from only selective circumstances. But unlike his creation, God wastes *nothing*. He provides a positive opportunity in *everything*. No circumstance is so bad, no personality so twisted, no situation so perverted, no life so broken that he cannot or will not use it for his own good purpose.

My father worked as a pinsetter for a bowling alley in Ontario, Oregon, before it became automated. The bowlers never knew who he was. In fact, most were completely oblivious to his presence. Only his legs and arms could be seen as he moved from lane to lane to lane, picking up pins that had been knocked down.

God moves from life to life to life, picking up things that have been knocked down. He won't throw something away just because it's broken. Not a broken heart. Not a broken home. Not a broken body. Not even a broken promise. In God's sight every life has value. He will use the most evil of circumstances for good. He doesn't waste hurricanes, terrorist attacks, failed economies, abusive family members, or cancer.

Remember the stories of Bible heroes taught us in Sunday school? Noah and the flood? Joseph in the pit? David and the giant? Daniel in the lions' den? God rescued each of them for one purpose—to bring glory to himself. We are oh so quick to find someone or something to blame for our bad choices or bad circumstances. We are equally as quick to claim the credit for our good choices or good circumstances.

The first line of Rick Warren's best-selling book, *The Purpose Driven Life,* reads, "It's not about you." The last line of his book could have appropriately read, "It's all about him." Believe it or not, like it or not, want it or not—we really do live our lives and make our choices before an audience of ONE.

God doesn't waste anything and uses everything
to bring glory to himself.

ENDNOTES

1. Dan Story, *Christianity on the Offense: Responding to the Beliefs and Assumptions of Spiritual Seekers* (Grand Rapids: Kregel, 1998), 18–19.
2. Aleksander Solzhenitsyn, *Orthodox America* (Templeon: World, 1983), http://www.roca.org/OA/36/36h.htm.
3. J. R. Miller, *Time With God—The New Testament for Busy People* (Dallas: Word Publishing, 1991), 451.

LaVergne, TN USA
23 February 2010

173908LV00001B/107/P